ALSO BY KEVIN YOUNG

Dear Darkness
For the Confederate Dead
Black Maria
Jelly Roll
To Repel Ghosts: The Double Album
Most Way Home

AS EDITOR

John Berryman: Selected Poems
The Everyman Anthology of Blues Poems
Giant Steps: The New Generation of African American Writers

TO REPEL GHOSTS

TO REPEL GHOSTS

REMIXED FROM
THE ORIGINAL MASTERS

KEVIN YOUNG

ALFRED A. KNOPF, NEW YORK

2014

THIS IS A BORZOI BOOK
PUBLISHED BY ALFRED A. KNOPF

www.randomhouse.com/knopf/poetry

Originally published in different form by Zoland Books, Cambridge, Mass., in 2001.

Library of Congress Cataloging-in-Publication Data
Young, Kevin.
To repel ghosts : remixed from the original masters / Kevin Young.— 1st ed.
p.   cm.
ISBN 0-375-71023-X (tr. pbk.)
1. Basquiat, Jean-Michel—Poetry.   2. Artists—Poetry.   I. Title.

PS3575.O798T6 2005
811'.54—dc22
2005040841

Manufactured in the United States of America
Published October 4, 2005

TO REPEL GHOSTS

[THE REMIX]

This remix was first conceived in the summer of 1999.
The double album version of *To Repel Ghosts* had been com-
plete enough to circulate since 1997, yet couldn't get airplay. In
between bouts of wanting to burn the masters, or throwing
the whole out the window, I came up with a more danceable
remix version like the one here.

When a publisher agreed to do *Ghosts,* I decided—having
told no one about my alternate take—to do the fuller, 350-
page epic, its breadth alone matching the prolific (and some-
times prodigal) nature of the late artist Jean-Michel Basquiat
himself. Since then, the remix has increasingly seemed to me
to deserve an airing—all the more so because it had its origins
in an earlier moment, and not in hindsight. So here it is, much
as I first recorded it, with a couple of bonus tracks not found
even on the "double album."

Perhaps it is not necessary to say this in a time of multiple
cuts and endings, but please note that this remix should not
be considered an afterthought, or replacement of the double
album, but rather an alternate take that's still the same song.
Different riffs. Either mix might serve as the first book in
Devil's Music, an American trilogy that continues in *Jelly Roll*
and ends with *Black Maria.*

Thanks for listening.

—THE MANAGEMENT

TRACKS

FAMOUS NEGRO ATHLETES

QUALITY MEATS FOR THE PUBLIC

b/w

SIDE B

MOST YOUNG KINGS
GET THEIR HEAD CUT OFF

NEGATIVE

Wake to find everything black
what was white, all the vice
versa—white maids on TV, black

sitcoms that star white dwarfs
cute as pearl buttons. Black Presidents,
Black Houses. White horse

candidates. All bleach burns
clothes black. Drive roads
white as you are, white songs

on the radio stolen by black bands
like secret pancake recipes, white back-up
singers, ball-players & boxers all

white as tar. Feathers on chickens
dark as everything, boiling in the pot
that called the kettle honky. Even

whites of the eye turn dark, pupils
clear & changing as a cat's.
Is this what we've wanted

& waited for? to see snow
covering everything black
as Christmas, dark pages written

white upon? All our eclipses bright,
dark stars shooting across pale
sky, glowing like ash in fire, shower

every skin. Only money keeps
green, still grows & burns like grass
under dark daylight.

PORTRAIT OF THE ARTIST
AS A YOUNG DERELICT

PAY FOR SOUP

BUILD A FORT

SET THAT ON FIRE

[JMB]

CAMPBELL'S BLACK BEAN SOUP

Candid, Warhol
scoffed, coined it
a nigger's loft—

not The Factory,
Basquiat's studio stood
anything but lofty—

skid rows of canvases,
paint peeling like bananas,
scabs. Bartering work

for horse, Basquiat churned
out butter, signing each
SAMO©. Sameold. Sambo's

soup. How to sell out
something bankrupt
already? How to copy

rights? Basquiat stripped
labels, opened & ate
alphabets, chicken

& noodle. Not even brown
broth left beneath, not one
black bean, he smacked

the very bottom, scraping
the uncanny, making
a tin thing sing.

POISON OASIS {1981}

Such church hurts—
all haloes, crowns,
coins ancient,

flattened. Cross-
roads. Money changes
hands stained

like glass. Mirror,
mirage—the dog
a praying mantis at his

feet. Basquiat eyes
the needle, needs
a fix—if the camel fits—

heaven. *Gimme*
some smack
or I'll smack

you back. Which side
should he pierce,
where to place

the dromedary
in his vein? Each opening
fills with wine

a wound. Hollowed
ground. Blood
of our blood—

Basquiat trades
Golgotha, skulls
& all, for an armful

of stigmata.
Runs a game,
plays snakes

& ladders, shooting
up. SAMO says: IF SOMEONE
SMITES YOU, TURN

THE OTHER FACE.
Even falling
has its grace—injection

& genuflection
both bring you
to your knees,

make you prey.

CADILLAC MOON {1981}

Crashing
again—Basquiat
sends fenders

& letters headlong
into each other,
the future. Fusion.

AAAAAAAAAA.

Big Bang. The Big
Apple, Atom's,
behind him—

no sirens
in sight. His career
of careening

since—at six—
playing stickball
a car stole

his spleen. Blind
sided. Move
along folks—nothing

to see here. Driven,
does two Caddys
colliding, biting

the dust he's begun
to snort. Hit
& run. Red

Cross—the pill-pale
ambulance, inside
out, he hitched

to the hospital.
Joy ride. Hot
wired. O the rush

before the wreck—

each Cadillac
a Titanic,
an iceberg that's met

its match—cabin
flooded
like an engine,

drawing even
dark Shine
from below deck.

FLATS FIX. Chop

shop. Body work
while-u-wait. *In situ
the spleen*

or lien, anterior view—
removed. Given
Gray's Anatomy

by his mother for recovery—

151. *Reflexion of spleen*
     turned forwards
     & to the right, like

     pages of a book—
     Basquiat pulled
     into orbit

     with tide, the moon
     gold as a tooth,
     a hubcap gleaming,

     gleaned—Shine
     swimming for land,
     somewhere solid

     to spin his own obit.

BROTHERS SAUSAGE {1983}

The trees told nobody
what, that day, we did—
we died. Laid down

with our cans
of deviled
ham & closed

our eyes—two
valises full
of Van Camp's

Pork & Beans—
the city an idea
shining far behind—

& we were not afraid

just terrified
of bears, of basic
black—the night—

white hunters
with their plaid
& pop-guns—

sleep was our bag—
a body—we began
to crave our beds

even empty & unmade
as a mind—
the silence & sounds

of nature scared us—

WORLD WORLD
FAMOUS—
EST 1897

COTTON,
SLAVES, IN MAY A
DERANGED—

this Indian
land given
no heed, taken

back & turned to park—

BEEF PORK SALT
WATER CORN
SYRUP SOLIDS

guns loaded
like a question,
aimed—imagine—

*shhhh—be vewy
vewy quiet, we're
hunting wabbits—*

DARWIN.
ALLAH. BUDDHA.
BLUE RIBBON.

MALCOLM X
VS. AL JOLSON—
whistling Dixie,

we pack up
like meat—ACME—
to the city—

CITY-AS-SCHOOL

Day-trips
in Washington Sq
Park, dropping

out—STONED
ON SAMO. Two hits
of acid a day

& each night
his father Gerard
worrying. Searches

the weeks high
& low. Finds his son
deep in a dice

game with God.
Blood
shot. Drags Basquiat

like a cigarette
back to Bklyn
to his high school

in the city—
"Papa I'll be very very
famous one day"

delirious Basquiat
declares. Hard
headed, mama's boy,

spleenless—
on a double
dare from Al Diaz,

fills a box with Papa's
shaving cream,
at graduation giving

Principal a white face
full of menthol.
NO POINT

IN GOING BACK — smart
ass Basquiat empties
his locker, heads

for the big city
with Papa's cash
loan. GOOD PLACE

FOR A HANDOUT.
EASY MARK
SUCKER. SURVIVING

CHILD WITH SEED OF LIFE—
knows only how to move
forward like a shark

or an 8-track, going
out of style. For broke.
PLUSH SAFE HE THINK:

Only the good
die numb—Bird
& Billie & Jimi

& Jesus—
his heroes
crowned

like a tooth.
GOLD WOOD.
Basquiat begins

with hisself, writes
FAMOUS
NEGRO ATHLETES

on downtown walls,
spraying SAMO
across SoHo—

"royalty, heroism
& the streets"—
covering galleries

with AARON
& OLD TIN. ORIGIN
OF COTTON. NO

MUNDANE OPTIONS.

MAN-MADE

WELL
  KEPT
    WHITE

CADILLAC—
  Basquiat dead
    broke on Saint

Mark's, marketing
  his postcards
    like coke

AN ADVERTISEMENT
  FOR SODA
    crashing out

at friend's pads,
  wherever he can.
    THIS GRAPH SHOWS

A TRIPLING OF FIVE
  TO SIX MILLION
    NEW

AND EXISTING UNITS
  WITHOUT PLUMBING.
    Crammed with pals

in photo booths
  taking shots
    WE HAVE DETERMINED

THE BULLET WAS GOING
  VERY FAST—collages
    the Warren Commision,

THE TEAM: RUNS
    HITS
        ERRORS.

Tries to hock
    his J. Edgar Hoover,
        Jack Ruby shooting

or a postcard flag
    to Henry Gedzahler
        & Andy Warhol

lunching
    at WPA—
        Too young

is all the cultural
    commissioner offers—
        IT TOOK THE GUILT

OF 4 GENERATION OF SWEATSHOP WORKER
    TO GAIN ACCESS
        TO THE STATESMAN—

but Warhol buys some dance.
    MILLIONAIRE$.
        15 PER CENT—

Here's a tip—
    sleep
        where you can

till they can't
    stand
        you no more—

cover the doors
   the fridge
      BEFORE THE CRANES

LIFT THEM
   OF THE EDGE
      OF THE 3-STORY

UNIT
   till slumlord
      tosses you out. LOVE.

A GIANT GORILLA
   LYING
      ON THE PAVEMENT.

His name not yet
   nailed up,
      neoned, across town

or bannered
   on the backs
      of bi-planes—

he hustles sweat-
   shirts hand
      painted—abstract

on front
   MAN-MADE©
      in back.

Cooks up schemes
   like stash.
      Technician

mad scientist
    scorcerer's apprentice—
        SAMO© must be

a white cat, they say,
    some conceptual artiste—
        couldn't be B,

this black kid in a lab
    coat & blond
        mohawk

with afro in the back—
    SAMO© AS AN END
    2 BOOSH-WAH-

ZEE FANTASIES—
    his arrow-head
        or weathervane

pointing out—away—

NEW YORK BEAT {1980–81}

Glenn O'Brien, dir.
Maripol, prod.

Gone from TV
Party to Great Jones
from special guest

to star, he's hooked
up—his first
crash pad—

the film's production
office. Catches sleep
like fire—PAY

FOR SOUP—
wakes to paint, playing
a day in the life

of artist
to the hilt. TILT—
his name up in

lights, smoke, the script
improvised, pin-
balled along. Body

English. MATCH.
Racks up
canvas & art

supplies—BUILD
A FORT—
trying to score

the ladies—
no dice. Add coins
to play. FIRST

AMBITION FIREMAN

FIRST ARTISTIC
CARTOONIST.
Among Blondie & electric

boogaloo, lies
his big break—head
spinning—scratch—able

to buy paint, a bit
of pot—he's stoked
SET THAT

ON FIRE—& some start
to notice. Blondie
buys her a small canvas

& he's dancing
with zoot-
suited, mustachioed

Kid Creole, making eyes
at the beached
Coconuts—brown out

& white inside—
cool as milk.
APOSTLE, ROT,

LIKE AN IGNORANT
EASTER SUIT.
He's busting up

& out, till the Italian
backers go bankrupt—
THE WHOLE LIVERY

LINE BOW LIKE
THIS—losing his roof
his flophouse fee, left

B holden
the bag. All that's kept
are some stills

& Maripol's Polaroids
of him shimmer
-ing—the film

SELF-PAINTINGS 6AM
like life
left unfinished.

BEYOND WORDS

Mudd Club 4th floor gallery
Manhattan, April 1981

If you bomb
the IND
or tag the 2

downtown
—gallery-bound—
dousing it in tribal

shrapnel, you're it
—the shit—
If you can lie

between the rails
—Please Stand
Clear the Closing—

or press yourselves
betw. train
& the wall

spray can rattling
like a tooth—*The roof*
the roof

the roof is on
fire—soon
the 6 will whistle

past, swinging
like a night stick—
Officer Pup throwing

a brick
@ that Mouse
Ignatz, in love —

#$!?!!!! — then
you'll have found
risk. A calling —

Crash, Daze, Pray
covering trains
like cave paintings,

avoiding the German
shepherds — ACHTUNG —
while the cars sit

in the yards
— what no one else in this
city owns. Making

their names
known — Dondi, Boy-
5, B-Sirius, Crazy

Legs, Coolie C —
The city clears
its throat

the subway shaking
the buildings above —
We don't need

no water let
the motherfucker
burn — Futura 2000,

Phase 11, Quick
& Sex & Zephyr
& Lady Pink—

Fab 5 Freddy
(né Braithwaite)
saying everyone's

a star. "Rapture"—

the whole planet's in
on it—Chilly Most
Being the Host Coast

to Coast—Freddy's painted
Campbell's Soup Cans that read
DADA & POP instead

of beef barley—
the UFO has landed
& a brother's

stepped out, alien, dressed
in white. *Then when*
there's no more cars

he goes out at night
& eats up bars—
graffiti like 3 card monte—

running, avoiding the pigs
like a black muslim
bean pie. *DJ spinning*

says my my.
Pay attn.—
say, ain't that

Basquiat spinning

disks behind Blondie —
SAMO© AS AN END
TO MINDWASH RELIGION —

45s stacked high
as a Dag-
wood sammich?

Hungry, this B-
boy's headed
to the top — *Yes*

Yes y'all
You don't stop —
blowing up.

DEFACEMENT {1983}

acrylic & ink on wallboard
25 x 30 in.

Basquiat scrawls
& scribbles, clots
paint across

the back
wall of Keith Haring's
Cable Building studio—

two cops, keystoned,
pounding a beat,
pummel

a black face—scape
goat, sarcophagus—
uniform-blue

with sticks. The night
Michael Stewart snuck
on the tracks

& cops caught him
tagging
a train—THIRD RAIL

DANGER LIVE
VOLTAGE—
taught him better

than to deface public
property. Choke
hold. Keep NEW YOKE

CITY Clean.
Give those men
a PABST BLUE

RIBBON, a slap
on the wrist
a meddle

of honor. Basquiat
produces *Beat
Bop*, black

on black
vinyl—VOCAL.
TEST PRESSING.

INTESTINES.
TARTOWN
RECORDS. EAR.

All revolutions
33 1/3.
When Haring moves

up & out, he'll tear
down that wall
careful to get

Basquiat out intact—
in Haring's
bedroom modeled

after the Ritz
¿DEFACEMENT?
sits, saved

like a face, framed—

RINSO

Grace—that's Miss
Jones to you—
done up

like the devil, old
Kali. Collared,
leopard

skinned—crouched
in a cage
her white photographer

& husband, placed
her in. Big
game. THE MOST

AMAZING DEVELOPMENT
IN SOAP
HISTORY. Butcher,

Maker, Josephine Baker
walked her leopards,
leashed, down

the Champs-Elysées
head high. KINGFISH.
SAPPHIRE. *I'm not*

perfect
but I'm perfect
for you—keeping

up, Jones goes
wild like a card.
Spade. THEM

SHOVELS. Joker,
queen, deuce
deuce—face

painted blue
by Warhol, her body
done in

white by Haring—
same as Bill T
Jones (no reln)

his cock striped
white, skunked.
Vein.

What a doll—
she wants to wear
Haring's radiant

babies, pale crosses,
tribal headdress
& all, to the ball. Little

else. Cinder-
ella has nothing
on Grace—

NO SUH
NO SUH
princess

& step-
sister rolled
into one. IL FOOL.

SLOGAN.
If the soft
shoe fits . . .

Diva, devil
may care—
she's riding high

as fashion. *Love
is the drug
& she's here*

to score.
(~~SAPPHIRE©.~~)
Slave

to the rhythm, rinse
—repeat—WHITE
WSHING ACTION—

DOS CABEZAS {1982}

*former collection
of Andy Warhol*

Cabezas means friends
or so we thought—the gap
in Basquiat's teeth

What me worry?
a generation
between both men—

Warhol with hand raised
pensing or perhaps
picking his nose—

Basquiat's snout flat
broad brushstrokes, hair
bushy. Right after

meeting official Warhol,
B headed
back home to paint

the pair, returning
to Andy's Factory,
the canvas still wet

as a kiss. A gift. Sold
at auction their faces fetch
five times the asking—

feeding frenzy
over the newly
& nearly

dead—*Do I hear
a hundred thousand*—
not two friends

we learned
but two—translated—
heads.

VNDRZ {1982}

Antennae, antlers,
rabbit ears
for better reception—

Basquiat's hair
a bundle of dread-
locks, coiled, clenched

in two fists
above his head.
A matador's hat.

No pick, no make
up, just a shark
skin suit on a throne

that's held half
of Harlem—a Siamese
on his lap,

looking sidelong.
MOST YOUNG KINGS
GET THEIR HEADS

CUT OFF. No coon-
skin coats
or homemade back

drops, JMB
sharp & wrinkled
like VanDerZee's

ninetysomething
hands, head tucked
beneath a black

hood, the light,
shrouded—days
later agitates

in complete
dark—Basquiat
bobbing up

from chemicals
to the surface,
face forming

like a ghost—exposed
fixed, washed. Right
before the year buries

our photographer,
Basquiat paints
VNDRZ—his bouquet

of hands, a staff
of a man, rod
full of lightning

striking that
knotted, volted,
vaulted name.

THE FUN GALLERY

A buzz in the air
already, Basquiat
beaming. RAY GUN

set to stun
—maximum—a hold
up in this hole

in the wall,
a billion
paintings pinned

to dry wall
like butterflies,
stomachs. He's made it

all from scratch
& paint.
The work's too low

his dealer warned—
everything should be higher
to keep up

your prices,
speed. All night
the crowds line

outside like Disneyland
& love it. Taken
over Manhattan

he's King
Kong or Mighty Joe
Young, social

climbing—gone
from trains
to scale the Empire

State. Keeping most
of the show
for hisself, hitches

a limo to Bklyn
by dawn—the armored
car hour—up

early—or late—
as if to his own
funeral—

"Papa I've made it"

hugs & hands
him a blooming
bouquet.

JACK JOHNSON

1982, acrylic & oil paintstick on canvas

Jack decided that being a painter was less of a vocation than he had supposed. He would be a boxer instead. He had the punch; he had the speed; he was capable of moving half a second before trouble arrived in his neck of the woods.

[DENZIL BATCHELOR]
Jack Johnson & His Times

BLACK JACK {B.31 MARCH 1878}

Some call me spade,
stud, buck, black. That last
I take as compliment —

"I am black & they
won't let me forget it."
I'm Jack

to my friends, Lil'
Arthur — like that King
of England — to my mama.

Since I got crowned champ
most white folks would love
to see me whupped.

They call me dog, cad
or card, then bet
on me to win. I'm still

an ace & the whole
world knows it. Don't
mean most don't want

me done in. But I got words
for them too — when I'm through
most chumps wish

they were counting
cash instead
of sheep, stars. I deal

blows like cards —
one round, twenty
rounds, more. "I'm black all

right & I'll never let them
forget it." Stepping
to me, in or out

the ring, you gamble—
go head then dealer,
hit me again.

And there had come into prominence a huge negro, Jack John-
son, who was anxious to fight Burns. In England we had hith-
erto heard very little of Johnson. He was three years older
than the white champion, stood 6 feet and one-half inch, and
weighed 15 stone. He appears to have started his career in
1899, and from that year down to December, 1908, when he
finally succeeded in getting a match with Burns, he had fought
sixty-five contests, half of which he won by means of a knock-
out. . . . He was very strong, very quick, a hard hitter, and
extraordinarily skilful in defence. He was by no means unintel-
ligent, and not without good reason, was regarded generally
with the greatest possible dislike. With money in his pocket
and physical triumph over white men in his heart, he dis-
played all the gross and overbearing insolence which makes
what we call the buck nigger insufferable.

[BOHUN LYNCH]

KNUCKLES & GLOVES, 1923

THE UPSET {26 DECEMBER 1908}

"Who told
you I was yellow?"
I wanted to know

taunted— "Come
& get it
Lil Tahmy"

in my best English
accent, inviting
Burns to dodge

my fists the way
he'd avoided me,
running

farther—Britain
France—than
that kangaroo

I once bet I could
outdistance & did.
Chased down

to Sydney
Stadium, now was nowhere
to go—no more

color line to hide
behind, no lies bout
my coward streak—

I will bet a few plunks
the colored man
will not make good!

That I wasn't game.
Baited him
like a race—first

round he fell
with his odds,
favored. By two

all bets were even
& I made him pay—drew
blood—pounded

his face into morse, worse
than what Old Teddy
Roosevelt could stand

to hear over the wire. Bully.
"You're white, dead
scared white

as the flag of surrender.
You like to eat
leather?" By twelve I bet

he wished
he was still
at sea, had stayed Noah

Brusso, not Burns
trapped in Rushcutters Bay
about to be smoked

like my finest
cigar. "Didn't
they tell us this

boy was an in-
fighter?"
By thirteen

rounds he bites
luck & dust —
the police

rush in like fools,
angels, afraid
for both of us

treading this ring
like water,
my wide wake.

There is no use minimizing Johnson's victory in order to
soothe Burn's feelings. It is part of the game to take punish-
ment in the ring, and it is just as much part of the game to take
unbiased criticism afterwards in the columns of the Press. Per-
sonally I was with Burns all the way. He is a white man, and so
am I. Naturally I wanted to see the white man win.

[JACK LONDON]
JACK LONDON REPORTS

THE CROWN {4 JULY 1910}

In order to take
away my title
Jeffries—Great White

Hope—emerged
like a whale, lost
weight, spouted

steam. Said Negroes
have a soft spot
in our bellies

that only needs
finding. Bull's
eye. He refused

our pre-fight shake—
my eyes clear
like the time, years

later, I saw Rasputin
at the Czar's Palace
weeks before the Reds

stormed in, & knew that big
man—whom no one could
outdrink or talk—was grand

but finished. Heard
it took five tries
—poison, stabbing, more—

before he went at last
under. Jeffries was cash
by round one. Fresh

from his alfalfa
farm retirement,
only he was fool

or good enough
to challenge me, stage
a bit of revolution—

the Whites
couldn't have
me running

their show, much less
own the crown.
Called for my head.

"Devoutly hope
I didn't happen
to hurt you, Jeff"—

my fists harpoons,
hammers of John
Henry gainst

that gray engine
—*I think I can*—
steaming. Stood

whenever in my corner
facing the sun
after giving him

the shady one.
My trunks navy
blue as Reno

sky, Old Glory
lashed through
the loops—that Independence

Day, despite warning
shots & death threats
before the match,

I lit Jeffries like black
powder, a fire
cracker—

on a breakfast
of 4 lamb cutlets,
3 eggs, some steak

beat him till he
hugged me
those last rounds

& I put him
out his misery.
You could hear the riots

already—from Fort
Worth & Norfolk,
Roanoke to New

York, mobs
gather, turning
Main Street into a main

event, pummeling
any black cat
who crosses

their paths.
Neck tie
parties—cutting

another grin
below any raised
Negro chins—

JOHNSON WINS
WHITES LYNCH
70 ARRESTED

BALTIMORE
OMAHA NEGRO
KILLED—

all because I kept
their hope
on the ropes. His face

like newsprint
bruised. On account
of my coal-fed heart—

caboose red
& bright
as his—what wouldn't give.

Amaze an' Grace, how sweet it sounds,
Jack Johnson knocked Jim Jeffries down.
Jim Jeffries jumped up an' hit Jack on the chin.
An' then Jack knocked him down agin.

The Yankees hold the play,
The white man pull the trigger;
But it makes no difference what the white man say,
The world champion's still a nigger.

TRADITIONAL

THE RING {13 MAY 1913}

The bed is just
another ring I'd beat
them white boys in—

double, four
poster, queen.
I'd go the rounds

with girls who begged
to rub my head
cause it was clean

shaven, polished.
Said it felt like billiards
to them, bald

black. Balling
was fine, but once
I began to knock out

their men & sweep
the women off their feet
—even bought one a ring—

well, that was too much.
When I exchanged vows
with my second wife

—before God & everyone—
they swore I'd pay. Few
could touch me anyway,

what did I care. Later
when she did herself in
in our bed, I knew

—sure as standing—
they'd pushed her
to the edge. After

I mourned & met
my next love
& wife—my mama,

Tiny, said
little but worry—
they trumped

up charges, 11 counts
of the Mann Act
so I couldn't fight. My dice

role came up thirteen—
a baker's dozen
of prostitution & white

slavery—a white jury
after one hour found me
guilty of crimes

versus nature. Put
me through the ringer.
Nigras, you see, ain't

supposed to have brains
or bodies, our heads just
a bag to punch. But I beat

the rap without fists—
disguised as a Black
Giant, I swapped

gloves—boxing
for baseball—traded
prison stripes for Rube

Foster's wool
uniform. Smuggled
north into Canada

like chattel, we sailed
the *Corinthian*
for England, staying below

deck. Fair France
greeted me with a force
of police—turns out to tame

the cheering crowds—
granted me amnesty,
let me keep my hide

whether world
champ, con, or stripped
like my crown.

Jack Johnson's case will be settled in due time in the courts. Until the court has spoken, I do not care to either defend or condemn him. I can only say at this time, that this is another illustration of the most irreparable injury that a wrong action on the part of a single individual may do to a whole race. It shows the folly of those who think that they alone will be held responsible for the evil that they do. Especially is this true in the case of the Negro in the United States today. No one can do so much injury to the Negro race as the Negro himself. This will seem to many persons unjust, but no one can doubt that it is true.

What makes the situation seem a little worse in this case, is the fact that it was the white man, not the black man who has given Jack Johnson the kind of prominence he has enjoyed up to now and put him, in other words, in a position where he has been able to bring humiliation upon the whole race of which he is a member.

[BOOKER T. WASHINGTON]

for United Press Association

23 October 1912

Some pretend to object to Mr. Johnson's character. But we have yet to hear, in the case of white America, that marital troubles have disqualified prizefighters or ball players or even statesmen. It comes down then, after all, to this unforgiveable blackness. Wherefore we conclude that at present prizefighting is very, very immoral, and that we must rely on football and war for pastimes until Mr. Johnson retires or permits himself to be "knocked out."

[W. E. B. DU BOIS]

CRISIS, August 1914

THE FIX {5 APRIL 1915}

That fight with Willard was a fix
not a faceoff. Out of the ring
three years, jonesing

for the States, I struck a deal
to beat the Mann
Act—one taste of mat

& I'd get
let back home.
But I even told

my mama—
Tiny,
Bet on me.

Once in the bout—run out
of Mexico by Pancho
Villa himself—I fought that fix

the way, years back, Ketchel
knocked me down
even after we'd shook

& agreed I'd take the fall
if he carried me
the rounds without trying

to ko—crossed,
doubled
over, I stood up & broke

his teeth like
a promise. At the root.
On the canvas

they shined, white
as a lie. But with Willard
that spring, each punch

was a sucker, every round
a gun. Loaded. Still
I fixed him—strung

him along the ropes
for twenty-five
rounds. At twenty-six

the alphabet in my head
gave way—saw
my wife take the take,

count our fifty grand
& leave. Did the dive,
shielding my eyes—

not so much from Havana
heat—its reek my favorite
cigar—as from the ref's count.

Down, I counted too, blessings
instead of bets. Stretched
there on the canvas

—a masterpiece—stripped
of my title, primed
to return to the States.

Saved. Best
believe I stood up
smiling.

If you tonight suddenly should become full-fledged Americans; if your color faded, or the color line here in Chicago was miraculously forgotten: suppose, too, you became at the same time rich and powerful;—what is it that you would want? What would you immediately seek? Would you buy the most powerful of motor cars and outrace Cook County? Would you buy the most elaborate estate on the North Shore? Would you be a Rotarian or a lion or a What-not of the very last degree? Would you wear the most striking clothes, give the richest dinners and buy the longest press notices?

[W. E. B. DU BOIS]

CRITERIA OF NEGRO ART

LAST CHANCE

Bought art
by the armful
—going out

of style
or mind—stocked
the bar full

& hired girls—
colored, white, some
you could hardly

tell—to serve
drinks & dance. Ragtime
bands, Dixieland

& a few Rembrandts
hung beside prizebelts
wide as my smile.

Hosting, hustling,
chryselephantine,
I dressed to the nines—

linen suits, white
ties, crocodile
shoes—the South

Side never saw
such finery.
Haberdashery.

Back then in
my Café de Champion
I could really put them

back—when the Levee
heard about my high
life, they demanded

prohibition, declared
us sin—wanted
to flood us out

the way Galveston, diluvian,
once tried to do me.
Still Bricktop sang nightly—

till some musician
shot me over
a white woman

whom I matrimonied
3 mos. later—
Where's your mother

Mrs Johnson? the press
pressed her. Her answer—
"I don't know

& don't care." They went after me
with a vengeance
—lock, stock, gun

barrel—so I left
that claw-patch
of crabs, Chicago,

& went abroad, nephew
& wife
by my side. We Three

Musketeers—redoubtable—
stuck out
& stuck it out

for years—leashed
leopards—run out of more
countries than I could

count, score
of suitcases
in tow. The Great War

pushed us to Mexico
City—we drank
with generals, *científicos,*

Presidents soon deposed—
forced again north
Tijuana way

to start my Main Event
Café. Soon I tired
of opening

wine, a life of cork—
vinegared
on prizefights

& bulls & bribes—
I wanted Chi-town
back, all that

jazz. Bid
freedom farewell
at the Last Chance

Saloon, grinning, shaking
hands with arresting
officers over

the border—then faced
Stateside the same judge
who'd given me a year

& a day. *You play*
square with me,
Jack & you won't find

things too bad
said Warden
(former Governor

of Nevada, where I'd bettered
Jeffries so bad
the fight film is still banned

blockaded).
To jail
I chauffeured myself.

In the Walls
at Leavenworth
I kept cigars

& liquor & my own
private cook—fought
all-comers & Topeka

Jack Johnson—spoke
on Job, Esau, Esther,
Revelations & the virtues

of a life of moderation.
"I was always
attacking—my attack

was to counter
the leads I forced."
Homilectics

got me let out early
—caught to NYC
the 20th Century

Ltd.—engineered—
steamed—running
on good behavior.

After his high society white wife committed suicide in a cafe
he owned in Chicago, Johnson married another white
woman—it was no coincidence. But one could question the
frame-up he faced. I mean, Jack Johnson being convicted of
violating the "White Slavery Act" and being sentenced to a
year and a day imprisonment . . . But exiled to Paris with joy—
and as usual "Very Grand." It had to be Europe and they say he
had a pet leopard he'd walk while drinking champagne with
crowds following.

[MILES DAVIS]
JACK JOHNSON Liner Notes

EXHIBITIONS

Ticker tape rain
up in Harlem—
my welcome

felt like freedom
after the tuck-tail
of jail. The day's news

tossed at my feet
the stocks
bonds. Outside

I toured my bass
viol, upright,
playing by ear—wrestling

pythons—selling
ointments & appearances,
Even spoke to a klavern

of Ku Klux
on the golden rule.
Their ovation after

sounded like Spain
& France, the crowds
who applauded

when I fought foes
who never stood
a ghost

of a chance—Arthur Craven
poet & pugilist—
or 2 horses, charging,

held by my arms
padded, wrapped in steel
locks. With Paris

showgirls I showed
off my strength, hoisted
three at a time

over my rotting
smile. But polite
as she was Europa kept me

under her opera
glass—no surprise
a zeppelin only I could see

pursued me across London
with my white
Benz & wife

once the Great War
began. Between
sparring & bull

fights & my show
Seconds Out!
I offered to spy

for the States—or the highest
bidder—but the Continent kept on
serving me orders

to leave. Eviction.
Exile. I tired. Double
agent, ex-con

artist, champ
no longer, I retired
to the States that had tried

blindsiding me like my first
fight against the Giant
at the carny—come one

come all—pay
a worn nickel, win $5
—a fortune—if you last

3 rds. Still standing
by the 2d, I was
guided by the Giant

towards the tent
& his rube waiting
with a blackjack

—I put an end
to that. Quick. Left
his eye dark. Left

town to my own
applause
the way in 'fifteen

when Moran got a good one
in—though not
his Old Mary—

I clapped with my leather mitts
—congrats—
before—left arm broken—

my right broke his nose.
Freed, I had a fancy
to play Othello

—took a fourth
wife, white
—ended up

in film *False Nobility*
rolling my eyes
like cigars. I star

now in *Aida* as an Ethiopian
King. They have me
like Selassie, decked

out in skins. In stills
I bow—awkward—
to a blackface queen.

*Do they put you
in chains?*
"If they can get them

on me, okay & good,
but I got to show up
well—can't be

a ninny." *Do you yet
know your fate?*
"They take me up

to Memphis—not
Tenn., but the old
country—a prisoner. Boy,

I mean to struggle plenty."

It was on a hot day in Georgia when Jack Johnson drove into town. He was really flying: Zoooom! Behind his fine car was a cloud of red Georgia dust as far as the eye could see. The sheriff flagged him down and said, "Where do you think you're going, boy, speeding like that? That'll cost you $50!" Jack Johnson never looked up; he just reached in his pocket and handed the sheriff a $100 bill and started to gun the motor: ruuummm, ruummm. Just before Jack pulled off, the sheriff shouted, "Don't you want your change?" And Jack replied, "Keep it, 'cause I'm coming back the same way I'm going."

[WILLIAM H. WIGGINS, JR.]

THE BLACK SCHOLAR

THE RACE {D. 10 JUNE 1945}

Always was
ahead
of myself

my time.
Despised
by whites

& blacks alike
just cause
I didn't act right.

Gave Negroes
a bad name—
shame. Was

always a swinger
a fast talker—
my rights

the kind that broke
men's jaws.
Bigot laws.

Only good
Negro is dead
broke—if only you'd

bought less
cigars, suits
—they say—spent less

time chasing
ladies, racing
cars, goggles on

as if an aviator—
back when most
white men walked, not

to mention us. Some
nervous coloreds
half-hoped

I'd lose
so's not to prove
their race

superior
then act
like it—or not—

or out—or up-
pity, whatever
that means. The man

on the street
knows who
I am—no one's

Numidian, long
lost Caucasian
as whites claimed

once I won. I am pure
Caromontee stock.
Big bucks. I spent

my life fighting—
crossing color
lines I never drew

up, dreamt. I put
the race on
check — track — no Jack,

no Joe
Louis. My arms still
too short to go

gainst God—
on this last
road, old,

I will
speed, heading
not home

but to another
show & pot
of gold — too late

to see the truck
carrying what —
swerve —

"Remember
I was a man,
& a good one" —

in hospital
interns will think me
another fancy —

only the older doctor
shall know me — dying —
my Zephyr hugging

like an opponent
in the last round
this pole

of power—utility—
my black body
thrown free—

FAMOUS NEGRO ATHLETES

In those days I never had enough money to cover a whole canvas. I wouldn't be surprised if I died like a boxer, really broke, but somehow I doubt it.

[JEAN-MICHEL BASQUIAT]
"Report from New York: The Graffiti Question"

FAMOUS NEGRO ATHLETES

B anomaly—
anomaly he be—
caught between

a hock
& a hard race—
From the peak

you can almost see

the far
side of the river
Lights stretch

out suburban
satisfied
Black is this

season in
It goes
with everythin—

They know not
who he is because
he is not like

what ever they know—

Lashed
to the mast
the hero rides

past, ignoring
the sirens
steering by stars

& desire—
Only he can hear—
The others' ears

stuffed w/ cotton
so's not to listen—
What leads us

into the water we
inhale
as if air, smiling

whiles we die—
Bliss is this—
Is not his

luxury, no matter
how heavy
his pockets, how full

still no one will let
Gentleman Jack
Johns'n board this Titanic—

O how the ship will rock
when it meets
that giant block

of ice—doing
the Eagle Rock—
It's not what

you can see
—the white—
that kills, but what you cannot

AMATEUR BOUT

PSALM

Blood in his mouth
this morning, high
cotton, a prize

fight—trying
to beat this thing,
breathe easy

as money.
THIS IS NOT
IN PRAISE

OF POISON
ING MYSELF
WAITING FOR IDEAS

TO HAPPEN—MYSELF—
THIS   NOT
     IS

IN PRAISE OF POISON
THIS   IS NOT
         NON

He's full
as his notebook
—with worry

His mouth
shoots
off like craps

"ANDY'S TRAP
NO DICE
STRICTLY CASH

PAIGET WATCHES"
this sick counter
clockwork, up

& downers—

TRUE STORY

SHOT A FOOL'S
"SHOT A FOOL'S
HEAD OFF"!

~~JAIL LINGO~~
Now this shot
to his arm

's got him
possumed, doing
the rope-a-dope

A PRAYER

NICOTINE WALKS
ON EGG·SHELLS
MEDICATED

THE EARTH WAS
FOR LESS
FORMLESS VOID—

his furnaced
breath, his iron
lung

DARKNESS FACE
OF THE DEEP
SPIRIT MOVED ACROSS

THE WATER
AND THERE
WAS LIGHT

"IT WAS GOOD"©

BREATHING INTO HIS
LUNGS 2000 YEARS
OF ASBESTOS

WAX SEAL
LINE
STAMP

VERY OFFICIAL
"FOR THE SICKLES
FOR THE MATTOCKS

FOR THE FORKS
FOR THE AXES"
SHINING SHOE

IN ST LOUIS
THE NON POISONOUS
POISONED

SO SELF RIGHTOUS
NO ONE IS CLEAN
FROM RED MEAT TO WHITE

Sex smell
of the smoke-
house

Sauce stains
like paint
on pale aprons

THIS NOT IN PRAISE
OF ~~POISON~~
THE BIGGEST BUISNESS

UGLY, FAT LIKE A PIG

LOVE IS A LIE

LOVER = LIAR

NEON SHOE REPAIR
He alphabets
east — Ave A,
C, D —

LOTTERY
CANDY
MAGAZINES

CIGARS©
Got a late
night jones

Sleepwalks
awake, high-
strung

along the ropes —
come out swinging
"ARAB SINGING"

& prayer from above
EFFECTIVE 12:01 AM
Make the rounds

trying to score
a TKO, the gate
big as a welter

weight's — A MICKEY
FINN WITH
FUZZ ON IT IN

A TURKISH BATH
In this corner
of Loisaida

ROACH EGGS
    ROACH EGGS
        ROACH EGGS

            ROACH EGGS
he wants to strike
some blows

score that heavy belt

PEEL

NOT IN PRAISE
NOT IN PRAISE
OF POISON

He's off
like a bet—dime
bag, training

bag, punch
drunk & judy—
a hit—

THE CUSTOMER
IN NEW YORK,
CHICAGO, DETROIT

JUNK AND CIGARETTES

SAINT JOE LOUIS SURROUNDED BY SNAKES

BIP! SPLAT!
BOP!
EAST. The Harlem

HVYWT CHAMP
WORLD
taking

a whupping. DOES NOT
FIGURE
SOME EARLY LICK

MUST NOT YIELD.
One night only—
SCHH VS. SCH

SCHSCHMSCHM
SCHSCHM
SCHMELING, MAX—

Hindenberged
home, a hero.
Uber-

mensch.
©1936
KING

FEATURES
SYNDICATE—
Rematch

against Saint
Joe Louis,
the whole of Harlem

listening. All
or nothing.
1,000,000 YEN.

Y* BL*ST*D
SW*B
struck through,

crossed
out—combination,
jab, upper

hand. All the flags
of Harlem USA
raised

like fists.
Jubilee.
The Brown

Embalmer
in this corner
BOXED (X 3)

BOXEO

his gloves down.
CROWN.
Trainers round

his neck like towels
halo
hiss his cauliflower ear.

MONARCHS

Kansas City's Own
World Colored Champions

1920

Arumi	rf, 2b	
Blukoi, Frank	2b	Philippines
Carr, George ("Tank")	1b, rf	California
Curry, Reuben "Rube"	p	Kansas City
Drake, Bill "Plunk"	p, rf	Sedalia, Mo.
Hawkins, Lemuel "Hawk," "Hawkshaw"	1b	Georgia
Jackson		
Johnson, Oscar "Heavy"	c	Atchison, Kans.
Johnson, Roy "Bubbles"	2b	Detroit
Lightner	p	
McNair, Hurley "Bugger"	p, lf	
Mathol, Carroll "Dink"	2b	
Mendez, José "Mendy"	p, 2b, mgr	Cuba
Moore, Walter "Dobie"	ss	
Ray, Otto "Jaybird"	rf, c	
Rodriguez, J	c	Cuba
Rogan, Wilbur "Bullet Joe"	p, rf	Oklahoma City
Washington, "Blue"	1b	

1922

Allen, Newton "Colt"	2b	Austin, Texas
Anderson, Theodore "Bubbles"	2b	
Joseph, Walter "Newt"	inf	Muskogee, Okla.
Sweatt, Geo. "The Teacher"	1b, 2b	Humboldt, Kans.
Taylor, Big	p	
Williams, Henry	c	Oklahoma

Yokum   p   Ash Grove, Mo.

1925

Allen, Newt   2b
Rogan Bullet Joe   p
Williams, Henry   c
Young, Tom "T.J."   c   Wichita, Kans.

1927

Allen, Newt   ss
Everett   ss
Orange, Grady   utility

Young, Maurice "Doolittle"   p
Young, Tom   c
Young, William (Tom's brother)   p   Wichita

1929

Allen, Newt   2b
Rogan, Bullet Joe   cf, p, mgr
Young, Tom   c

1931

Allen, Newt   2b
Byas, Richard "Subby"   c, cf
Harris, Chick "Moocha"   p, lf

Stearnes, Norman "Turkey"   of   Detroit
Thompson, Samuel "Sad Sam"   p
Young, Tom   c

1932

Bell, James "Cool Papa"   of

1935

Allen, Newt   2b, capt
Brown, Willard "Big Bomb"   ss, 3b   Shreveport, La.
Kransen (Kranson, Cranston) Floyd   p

Rogan, Bullet Joe	utility	
Trouppe, Quincy	cf	Georgia
Young, Tom	c	

1936

Allen, Newt	2b	
Else, Harry "Speedy"	c, p	
Harris, Curtis "Popsickle" "Popeye"	1b, utility	
Paige, Leroy "Satchel"	p	Mobile
Webster	p	
Wilson, Woodrow "Bo" "Lefty"	p	

1937

Allen, Newt	2b	
Johnson, Byron "Jewbaby"	ss	
Mays (referred to as Ed, Tom, Dave)		

1938

Adams, "Packinghouse"	3b	
Allen, Newt	2b	
Bowe, Randolph "Bob" "Lefty"	p	
Jackson, "Big Train"	p	
Moses	p	Farmerville, La.
O'Neil, John "Buck"	1b, rf	Sarasota, Fla.
Strong, Ted	ss	Chicago

1940

Allen, Newt	2b	
Barnes, V.	of	Hub, Miss.
Matchett, Jack "Zip"	p	Odessa, Tex.

1941

Allen, Newt	ss, 3b, mgr	
Johnson, "Cliff" "Connie"	p	Stone Mountain, Ga.
Stong, Ted	3b, rf	

Young, Tom	c	

1943

Allen, Newt	utility	
Barnhill, David "Impo"	p	
Souell, Herbert "Baldy"	3b	

1944

Allen, Newt	1b, 1f	
Bumpus, Earl	rf	Kentucky
Rivers	cf	
Young, Edward "Ned" "Pep"	c	

1945

Gray	c	
Moody, Lee	1b, cf	
Paige, Satchel	p	
Renfroe, Othello "Chico"	lf, 2b	
Robinson, John "Jackie" (traded Brooklyn Dodgers)	ss	Cairo, Ga.
Young, Leandy	of	Shreveport, La.

Before Baird sold the franchise 1955, he sold
8 Monarchs to the majors & 4 to the minors.
The details of transactions not reported.

MUHAMMAD ALI BY ANDY WARHOL

1977, acrylic & silkscreen ink on canvas

Knockout—
looker, loose

talker. Your
mama.

Colorful
in Warhol

's red wash—
fists up

like pre-fight
predictions—

Ali fingers what rounds
his opponents

will go down.
Who knew when they paid

to see a fight
they'd see the launching

of a colored satellite!
Battled Frazier—

that ugly gorilla
(whose grandmother

had blond hair
down to here) enough

times to shorten both
their lives. Hospitalized.

Lips fat
as their bank

as bacon. Swelled
heads. His skin

tone brown,
even, mixed

by an assistant—
still the lips

are his, not stock
or air-

brushed. Full.
No smile.

CASSIUS CLAY BY BASQUIAT

1982, acrylic & oil paintstick on canvas

I'm pretty!
I shook up

the world! Clay shouts
to the announcer

after trouncing
Sonny Liston —

the next day he
will turn Ali.

Butterfly,
bee — none stung

or swole carpet-red
as the paint B covered

this canvas, drawing
blood — not even Cassius

called out his name.
Refusing to recognize

Allah — like Terrell
or fool Floyd Patterson —

will get you a new haircut,
whether you want one

or not. How
he hounds

Liston, waving
his prize belt —

a noose for Sonny's ex-
con neck. Petty crook.

Ali just bout serves
time himself

—title stripped
like paint

—Army taking away
his right to fight

when he won't fight
them Viet Cong

who've done him
nothing wrong.

Houston, we gots
a problem—will not

bow or stand
when his no-longer-

name the Draft
Board calls. Lords

over Liston
—*Get up, you bum!*

—who will fall to a phantom
punch 1st rd, forget

to get up. (Died,
Liston did, five

years later, in Vegas,
the needle in

his arm, the neon.)
Ali, now he could hit you

into next year—
but apart from the flogging,

his flaunting, were the taunts
challengers heard ringing

Uncle Tom! Come on
Come on White America!

even above the ten count
& crowd—his undented smile—

that smarts still.

IN ITALIAN

a trip

The West Indian posed as a prize fighter and made quite a few
lire letting much smaller and weaker Italian boxers knock him
out, while the crowd roared at the prowess of Italy. No doubt,
he is quite rich by now, this Negro, and is probably posing as
an Ethiopian, and still getting knocked out.

[LANGSTON HUGHES]
The Big Sea

THESIS 1983

Off the record, please—
Exhibit B
building up

his resistance—
"LUX LUCET IN TENEBRIS"
RED CROSS, PARKER

SOLO, BEGINNING OF—
getting a taste
of what's next—the fire

of time. IMPORTED MEAT.
Arsonist,
artist—a new lease

life. Search & destroy
deploying decoys
i.e. Trojan

Horse—CANINE
PRE MOLAR
SAME SIZE RIVER.

Crossed Rubicon
's cube, crossed
hisself holy—

MONA LISA
FALLING THE STAIRS
DOWN—

A

GOOD

PAINTING.

"PERFECT Δ
FROM EYES
TO CENTER

BREAST." Head
bobs on his chest
CLAY BUST

W/ THORNS—
a foreign needle
exchange student

enrolling this crash
& burn course. Europe
on $5000 a day

or less. Drum
talk, smoke
signals—INVENT

ENEMIES.
For Immediate
Release Please Post—

Low Boy
In Junkie Paradise
obeying LEAPSICKNESS

THE LAW
OF LIQUIDS —
go to lowest

point, & stay.

FLASH IN VENICE
  Like lightening
SHAZAM!
he zigzags

across Europa —
speed of sound,
light, speed

in hand swallowed —
run so fast
won't sink

in water, can
alter the atoms
in body & thus

walk through walls
— outrun bullet —
faster human eye.

Worried he's a flash
in the pan, an art
test dummy —

Draw "Tippy"
Turtle & send
us — Sketch famous

Draw Me Head
using pencil or pen
—We will judge—

2. Do you enjoy art
enough to want
to improve?

3. Did you study in
grade school?
4. Other art training
5. How much devote
each week?

7. Other members family
artistic?

    Like THOR
of North, found god
in a lightning rod—

a club—made his hair
grow. Now done
with blonde

he's moved on—fast
track—secret ID—
minus a mask

FALSE

ROMULUS + REMUS
saying uncle
uddering

under the she-wolf
—THEATER SEATS.
APHRODITE.

PERICLES. Perilous
road leads
him here—hunger

plan B on a crash
test diet—
delicious shakes

for breakfast lunch,
a sensible withdrawal
for dinner. Scars-

dale. Count
Chocula. BRUTUS AS
1ST CONSUL. Fiending—

B in need
of refreshdment
—the pillow mint

in the Ritz
—something to fill
his stocking

like coal. Black
Peter. Salt.
"PAX ROMANA"—

B in the head
losing his
—steers

that porcelain
bus—SANITIZED—
Do Not Disturb.

Et tu, Rufus?

TRUE FALSE
—his technicolor
yawn his just

say ahh
—wrecks his hotel
like a ship—

sunk. ROME IS SACKED
BY GOTHS.
—Does that Dick

Gregory dance
striking hunger.
—Does portraits

on a plate
then gives
them away—ANDY

WARHOL
"BOY GENIUS"
—PABLO PICASSO

(the eyes)
—FRANZ KLINE
with splashes

of black across
the fine white
chinette (all owned

by the Warhol Estate).
ALEXANDER
THE GREAT (X 2)—

B in the john
just saying
No—FALSO—

BARBARIAN
INVADER FOR THE FIRST TIME
SEES ROME

THE ITALIAN VERSION OF POPEYE
HAS NO PORK IN HIS DIET

Anchors
on the insides
of his arms

aweigh—
inked on
by needle

drill syringe—
wants spinach
without oink

greens minus
ham hocks
prosciutto

pepperoni
HOO
HOO HOOVES—

can lid flipped
open like Sailor Man's
one good looker

ahoy matey—
Sweepea, Olive
Oyl, a corn

cob pipe
puffing away
in his mouth

choo choo—
~~BUM~~ BUM
EAR—BRACCO

DI FERRE—
Bluto blottoed
ko'd, Wimpy

wanting a nickel
Will gladly pay
you Tuesday

for a hamburger today—
FOUR BIG
100% PERCENT.

He's strong
to the finish
cause he eats

him spinach—
able, again,
to save the day

POPEYE VERSUS THE NAZIS

KRYPTON.
A PLACE
TO MOVE

NEGROS.
COLORED PEOPLE.
FATS TRYING

TO ESCAPE
THE SKIN.
CADIUM. YELLOW

LIGAMENT.
TEN PER
CENT.

(PECHO.)
FAMOUS NEGRO
ATHLETES NO.

#47—
SPECIMEN.
BROOKLYN

DODGERS.
ELBOW
ELBOW BUST

OF A NEGRO—
UPPER TORSO.
(ERROR.)

ESOPHAGUS.
INTFERIORITY PLEX.
NECK. SCHIZOPHRENIC.

FATS TRYING TO ESCAPE
THE SKIN.
ULTRA HIGH

FUREQUENCY.
P. ROEBSON.
ACTION COMICS

AT HIS PRIME
—DYNAMIC—
CRISPUS ATTUCKS

HIGH. PREE
1951–1953
"CHEROKEE"

SWALLOWS IODINE?
¿POW?
BRUNO BELIEVE

SPINACH
IS POISON.
KRYPTONITE.

JIMMY OLSEN.
BERLIN 1936—
JESSE OWEN

CATHARSIS
What all
he's missing
—SPLEEN

LIVER LEFT
PAW. B been
losing it—fold

perforated line & tear
—SUICIDE ATTEMPT—
why not just

jump ship, swim
for it? He's tired
of this feeling

of feeling
a thing. THUMB.
ARM.

RADIUM. He's in
the dark, glowing
glowers. How

old it's grown—
IL MANO—
the fist made

of his THROAT.
His neck's guillotine
fit—perfect—

strains in the Sistine
Chapel to see
the gap between

God's hand
& human—torn
from his side.

SWALLOWS IODINE
Yardbird does,
not the first time

he inked his insides
& felt the dye
spread—cast—that feeling

again—DIZZY
ATMOSPHERE
ALL THE THINGS YOU ARE—

suffers
niggeritis—African
American sleeping sickness

~~FIRST DRAFT~~
FINISHED
PRODUCT—may

cause drowsiness.
Doses, dozes—FORTEZZA—
take 2 & call

it mourning.

PERUVIAN MAID
OR, 3/4 OF OLYMPIA MINUS THE SERVANT

    While in Europe
we heard this story, which
like all stories, is true:
a maid was hired in a hurry
to replace the well-loved, long-term,
live-in housekeeper
at the house we were staying in
for free—she'd cook
& clean & generally keep
up the place.
        A friend
of the family's, a kid
really, was having trouble:
his father drinking them
both dry. ABSINTH. Out of house
& home. Even money has its limits,
like men.
        One day, between drunks,
the father begged his son to save
them both, to go under
Lake Geneva & take
from their vault all he could
& sell it.
        The son did—
like anyone else would—found
row after row of paintings,
Mapplethorpes, even
that famous one of Warhol
pale, successful, eyes
closed, almost dead.
        We saw that
one ourselves, casually leaned
against the wall like a broom.
        Gathered
the father had been quite

a collector in the 80s
art boom bull
market & didn't even know
what he had.

        After counting
& cataloguing & asking
artwise friends what
the work was worth, the son sold
many pieces, mostly for cash. He kept
some *objets* at his friend's family
home—along with thousands
in Swiss francs—in order
not to tempt his father's
swimming will.

        One morning
while the son lounged,
sunning beside the family
friend's pool, the new maid
came out to ask—*en français*
no doubt—whether
he wanted anything
cool to drink.

        He did,
merci. She went inside again
only to rush
out to the driveway—he would
have said 'carport'—duck into
her subcompact, then zoom
backwards out the long, pebbly,
private drive. A little fast
for groceries, no? For
lemonade?

        Then it struck him—
rushed upstairs to check
his briefcase—gone

was the cash, every penny
—or is it *centime*—each
colored bill.
    The maid may not
have been Peruvian, but North
African or Senegalese,
less likely the shade
of Olympia's servant
than the color of Olympia
herself.
    They found her
car at the French border,
figured, back home, she could live
on the money for seven
years, ten. Well.
        What
would you have done? The money
there, mottled, still greener
than any future you had
imagined—despite creature
comforts of work, a roof.
        Back home
the family you hadn't seen
for years, father not growing
any younger, mother becoming
more bent.
        We each pay
in different ways: FROM THE VAPOR
OF GASOLINE Basquiat's maid said,
charcoal scrawl on slats of white wood.

FIRST CLASS {1983}

Untitled, *oilstick on paper*
50 x 96 1/2 in.

Lands
from the Concorde
unable to catch

a cab—REPLACEMENT—
MILK
BONES—SPIN

AL TAP.
10 MILES
FIVE MILES

20 MILES—
rainsoaked Basquiat
hails in vain—

COWBOY HAT
WAGE CONCESSION
CHINESE LABOR.

MICE. LARGE DOG.
UPPER TEETH AND JAW.
Hotshot

hopping mad, gracious
furious—
MOLTEN METAL

SOUTH. SOUTH.
UN BOMBERO
ERROR

ADMIRAL BYRD.
Walking
homeward, still waving

down the yellow
the checkered cars—
READING RAILROAD

SHORT
LINE RAILROAD
B & O—

COAL. Dreadlocks
drenched—A REAL
CHAMPION—but no one

stops.
Gives up.
RODENT FESTIVAL

UNION
PACIFIC CO.—
paint-wet Basquiat

hoofing it, catching
the subway
like a cold.

BEST REMEMBERED
AS JIMMY OLSEN.
Superman or super-

intendent—
1. MANUAL
2. ELECTRIC

don't matter
how much you makes,
what cut

your hair—
degraded Basquiat
has grown

used to this,
ingrate Basquiat
never—

~~THE USUAL~~

~~HORROR~~

~~STORY~~

BASEBALLS
MADE IN
HAITI—

BIG MAN IN A BLUE SUIT
AND THE END
OF THE 20TH CENTURY.

QUALITY MEATS FOR THE PUBLIC

As much as undervaluation can kill, so can a false sense of the value of your work. Jean-Michel was advised to stop giving it away. But if your friends can't have it, why live?

[RENE RICARD]

HOLLYWOOD AFRICANS {1983}

Basquiat paints

the town. PAW.
BWANA. SEVEN
STARS. Night

life—star-struck
Basquiat's arrived,
brought Toxic

& Rammellzee along
for the ride. Our trio
stomping new

ground—shaky,
kept. *Hills,*
that is—black

gold, Texas tea—
out west
Basquiat burns

his canvas ochre,
this trinity thin
as their ties. *Hip*

hop hippity hop—
Sunset Blvd
Walk of the Stars,

streets stretched
like limos. B
at last in the black,

dines out at Mr. Chow's.
IDI AMIN. 200 YEN.
Put it on his tab—

trading meals
for canvases free
loaded with msgs,

HERO-ISM.
TOBACCO in purple,
palimpsest. Toxic

& RMLZ cool, eyes
shaded by goggles,
hats with zs. Snores

ville. GANGSTERISM.
SELF-PORTRAIT
AS A HEEL #3. Hail,

hail, the gang's all
heels—no winners
or winters, just

wanderlust
amongst Oscars®
& MOVIE STAR

FOOTPRINTS
like an astronaut's.
Rock rock planet rock

don't stop—POP
CORN—SUGAR
CANE. Academy

Mammy Award
& another for Butler,
Rhett—To the moon

Jemima—PAW—
Basquiat rockets
NEW!—hands pressed

fresh into pavement,
permanent as a rap
sheet, booked.

SELF-PORTRAIT AS A HEEL, PART TWO

Brown
boy at the bar
downing tin

& gonics—
mixes his volatile
cocktail—one part

pain, the other
champ—
this bubblubling

in his nose—feeling
Live & Smokin'
like Rich-

ard Pryor, a stand-up
guy—he's been placed
on seven

second delay (just
in case he bleeps)
& not even known it

like the time Pryor was host

—no supper
no last request—
Live it's Saturday Nite!

He's only a guest.
Or samurai busboy, worse.
Your mamasan.

He spills like news
his drink, douses
hisself generous as Pryor

the brush fire
—Holy Moses, it speaks—
running down the street

racing like poor Jesse
Owens, late
in life, in the Hippodrome

—an exhibition—
versus
some heartwormed horse

COKE® {THE REAL THING}

His nose
is open—
he wants him

some white
girl, needs
to score—

Might want
to quit
her, but he's

an addick
& she's his dealer
& only takes

ten percent.
Says she'll hook
him up with Warhol— *White*

lines Blowin through
my mind
And now I'm having

fun baby—
Don't be so nosy,
he's got it under

control. Just a chippie.
Needs advice like another
hole in his nose—

done a job
on it already.
Snowed. Nose

blown & eroded
like the Sphinx,
his olfactory's gone

on strike
— to pot — scabs
brought in. White

collared crime.
Bidnessman is caught
with 17 kilos He's out

on bail & out of jail
& that's the way it goes —
On fire, cranks

out work
— Prometheus, epidermis —
ALAS; "WINGS"

MOSTLY BUZZARDS —
culture vultures
who swoop & swallow

studios whole,
day after day. *Huh —*
sugar — cane —

Some leave out
his place
with paint not dry yet

others give bills
he burns by
the hundreds

taking a lighter
to Ben Franklin's
face, kite flying

lightning. He's over
it all, pours
a still

life, basket
of nuts & fruit,
birdfood

dumped on the head
of the collector showing
off her black

chaffeur. Rochester—
Freeze—Rock—
smoke & mirrors

the funhouse
he snorts off—the dollar
the razor—dusted.

OXIDATION PORTRAIT OF JEAN-MICHEL BASQUIAT {1982}

How many people
    did Warhol pay
        or over lunch ask

to piss across
    the canvas,
        its silk-

screen of Basquiat,
    hair in Mickey
        Mouse knots?

How long
    till the urine
        fought

the copper
    paint, began
        to rust?

rot? before
    his portrait
        grew green

& gold, spotting
    his face
        like liver,

a leopard, like years
    later, spleen
        gone, the heroin

started to eat,
    stark communion,
        his skin?

TOXIC {1984}

CENTS in his
mouth like a scare-
crow stuffed

with news
print—a blanket
of words behind

him, infected,
undetected—hands
raised, braised

brown as turkey
legs. SMOKE
BOMB. SOUP

TO NUTS.
FIG 21—
EGG. Snake.

THAT EGG.
"BOY IT'S SURE
HOT HERE"—Bugs

Bunny, his goose
cooked over carrots—
GOLD. UNISON (INTRO)

all together now—
COMPOSED
TRUMPET SAX

(IMPROVED)—
his blue pork-
pie hat

a trumpet
muffler—
squealer. MILES

DAVIS. GREGOR
MENDEL INVENTOR
OF X-RAY—

blowing down trom-
bones. Half
lives. Old school.

Head spun—
an electron,
popping

locking, anti-
matter. Eureka!
DR RADIUM

turning lead
paint to oil,
gold

standard. Agent
orange.
Noble gas,

neon. Change
in his mouth
like a piggy bank

back, bills
piling up,
a beggar's dead

presidents
littering a hat—
VEHEMENT ALLEY CATS

GARBED A LA
KLU LUX KLAN PLAN
TO TORTURE THE—

notify next
of kin, a sign
on the doors

spare
our first born.
Hands raised—

a saint
or a sinner, holy
rolling.

Snake eyes.
Dice kissed
for luck—

"PORKY'S PIG FEAT"
RACKATEER RABBIT—
C'mon bones

baby needs
new shoes.
Just wave your hands

in the air!
Arms raised
in praise

or a stick up—
nobody moves
nobody hurt.

Around his cop-
colored, hip
hop top

hat, the halo
a cameo—
ODOURS OF PUNT.

    LACK
    OWDER
FROM AESOP'S

    ER   AND HIS CAT"—
blown up—
POOF—a hit

record, a vinyl
spill—
gone platinum.

INDUSTRY©.
I'm the King
of Rock

there is none higher—
a silent
canary down

a mine.
Drunk off
Molotov

cocktails—
moonshine. White
lightning. Acid

rain. 40 ounces
& a mule—
prescription,

placebo, he's out
to score
a fifth

of prevention,
a pound
of flesh. Antidote

anodyne—CENTS
in his mouth
like God's

unsaid name in a golem's—

VOCABULARIO

cabal
caballero
cacao

cadáver
café
cambio

¡caramba!
carbón
caribe

Carmen
carnaval
carnívoro

catecismo
célebre
celibato

censor
centrífugo
cerveza

César
cicatriz
ciudad

civilizacíon
combustible
complexión

cómplice
conductibilidad
corazón

corrosivo
cuba
chimpancé

chocolatería

ONION GUM {1983}

ONION GUM
MAKES YOUR
MOUTH TASTE

LIKE ONIONS
ONION GUM
MAKES YR MOUTH

TASTE LIKE ONIONS
INGREDIENTS:
ENRICHED FLOUR

Bunion gum makes
your mouth taste
like bunions

Bunion gum makes
your feet taste
like bunions

NIACIN, REDUCED IRON
Union gum
makes your

mouth taste
like Lincoln
Union gum

makes your mouth
head south
RIBOFLAVIN

engine engine
Injun gum
makes your

mouth taste
tobacco Injun
gum makes your

mouth taste
lottery
union gun

onion gun
Ink gum
makes your

mouth taste
calamari
Ink gum

makes your
mouth turn
negro

cuttle gum
colored gum
Bubble gum

makes yr mouth
pink & sore
Bubble gum

makes yr mouth
blow sugar
über gum

bazooka gum
THIAMINE
MONONITRATE

MADE IN JAPAN©
Redhot gum
makes yr mouth

taste like pepper
Redhot gum
makes yr mouth

taste like love
SNAKE
SERPENT

"HARMLSS"
ur-gum
anti-gum

ONION GUM
MAKES YR MOUTH
TASTE LIKE

ONIONS ONION
GUM MAKES
YOUR MOUTH

TASTE LK ONIONS

EYES + EGGS {1983}

Eats. Hot
cakes. Griddle
cakes. Silver

dollars. Head
cook, pepper-dark.
Dumb

waiter. Lazy
Susan. 24 SERVICE
24 SERVICE

24—
footprints
across a canvas

apron. Rice
in the salt
like luck, over

a shoulder. Marry
the ketchup.
Today Special—

grits, links,
sweetbreads.
This is your brain.

This your brain
on drugs, scrambled
with a side

of bacon, smiling.
Mouthless.
Black JOE.

A warmer?

Order up—
Adam & Eve
on a raft, tuna

on whiskey—
WERE HAPPY
TO SERVE YOU.

Wanted Help.
We're in the weeds—
come on back

now hear?
TO INSURE
PROMPTNESS 15%.

Two bits. End
of shift, punching
out. The whites

like an eye
—eighty-sixed—
sunny, pow-

dered, poached—

PORK

Ham, Sons of
Ham hock
Ham i.e. showoff

OLEO ·

Between Follies
the funniest
man alive

or dead, emerges—
his behind
feathered, legs

a rooster's—
Mama's Little Baby
Loves Shortenin

Shortenin
Mama's Lil Baby Loves
Shortnin Bread—

come a mighty long
way from Walker
& Williams'

Authentic Coon
Revue—Walker
the dancing dandy

& Wms in cork
for *Sons of Ham.*
OLEO. LARD. Hamming

it up. Now
for Ziegfield
Mr Williams eats

alone, not allowed
front doors
or full billing—

may bring the house
down, but must
come in the back—

a separate room,
nothing
personal, mind

you, just house
rules—where he puts on
his face—

TRICK BLACK SOAP.
In his own light
skin, he's no one's

idea of funny
—plain brown wrapper—
but blacked up

Uncle Eggs delivers—
does his olio
between the show

girls, all ostrich
& boas, gloves
mortician white,

sight
gags before curtains
these scalped seats.

QUALITY

POSTOAKOES
REST IN PEACE WHO TRUST?
WARM AIR FRONT

MASS SLUMS
CUTTHROATS
DUST BOWL

IDAHO
PUBLIC GHETTO
RIBS PORK

POPCORN
PER CAPITA
WHY VERSUS ROME.

QUALITY?
POLKA DOTS
IN PORT AU

PRINCE HAITI
PROPH E IES 59¢
GUILTY

200 BEATS PER MIN
E PLURIBUS
PILGRAMAGES

THIEVES
FROM THE MAYFLOWER
DISNEY©

1. STATUES
2. VENUES
JAMES VANDERZEE

POTATOES
CORN WHEAT
THE COTTON INDUSTRY

OF NINETEEN
THIRTY EIGHT
SHO'NUFF

JIFFY POP
DISPOMANIA
BANG POW

CRACK

REVISED UNDISCOVERED GENIUS OF THE MISSISSIPPI DELTA

Struggles
   up the stairs for days
      or they carry him

to the landing—once
   inside, he can't quite
      walk around his own

show at the Center
   for the New South—
      born into

slavery, bred
   a sharecropper,
      he spent all

his uncounted years behind
   mules who wouldn't move—
      He's sullin,

don't budge. Stayed
   put, laboring
      beneath the Belt

Black as a Bible.
   He storks
      across his exhibit

a hothouse flower
   or ostrich, saying
      little, slow steps

stilting the room.
   Walls teem
      with his silhouettes,

giant dogs.
  CATFISH.
    The ripe

cardboard canvases
  sun-browned
    primed

beside the old Coke
  machine.
    He seen

it all, enough—
  time
    to return

to his corner
  —the market—
    the young boys

who set a spell
  while he works—the white
    youth who stops by

& takes away
  Mr Traylor's art
    in exchange

for fresh cardboard,
  some oils.
    ~~CATFISH~~.

Thanks kindly. Traylor still
  prefers the old backings
    from men's shirts, the kind

the dead wear, across the street
    in the funeral parlor—
        where he, on his flat

pallet, sleeps.

RED KING

MAGI

A hard coming—crossing—
the days & desert—the dust
& the light. Nights bitter

as the inside of the moon.
But that bright! The glare
of it we couldn't stand

or reach. We rode. SPOONS
SHARPENED TO CUT
FLOUR WITH WHITE

LEAD. Arrived
grayed, bent,
& gave & gave. We kings.

Were.
The dusk among us then.
Gifted,

we should never have looked
that horse full in its mouth,
simply bowed among the cattle

the sheep, & believed.

CROWN

The King had his
hands full
with the Queen's be-

heading. The play,
the thang. Q: ARE NOT
PRINCES KINGS?

Get out, dear
dauphin, before
the mob tires

of yesterday's bread
before you become
yourself the mob—

& pitch & burn
you own
house down.

You can swim up
stream only
so long—

And out of the cane came
this man, "All
Saint," hallo-

we'ened, his machete
raised, cutting
down the crop which kept

each autumn coming.
A bayonet sea—
pure cane

sugar ganulated sifted
by the devil—
that sound in thee ears

the musket march
of March, L'Ouverture
songing bars

like jail, like court
martial, that humming
we need no tongue for,

that even gagged might muster.

NOD

He claimed a country—
his own—anatomy
of star & bone.

He called it home.
He bore the mark
& so would his sons

(he had none).
The King claimed a state
of emergency, a place

where the sick could get
help, where the help
never got sick. Kitchens

shone, spit & polish.
MOST YOUNG KING
S GET THEIR HEAD CUT OFF.

This one
wadn't that lucky.
He claim

a country like money
from a bet. Gentle-
men place your debt—

black red black red,
roulette—
He claim his country,

rainy though it may be.

NEW ART, NEW MONEY

> New York Times Magazine *cover story,*
> *February 1985*

Shoeless
like a '68 gold
medalist,

bronze. TIN.
ASBESTOS.
Fastest

in the world!
Poker-faced—
his brush raised

like cards, royal
flush, ace—
instead of black fist,

protest. Poster
boy wonder.
High roller—

his *Comme des Garçons*
uncivil suit
paint-splattered—

NO U S A
across his chest,
no suede

pumas—
just the *bête noire*
beside him

a silhouette mute
on silver,
grinning. New art

new monkey
on his back—
black

balled. Kick
backs. Who's got
the short end

of this shtick?
Basquiat, Inc
in hock

trying to sell
passersby a painting
for two dollars—

FLAT FEE. Eliminate
the middle
man. Hoodoo

economics—needs
FILTER
CIGARETTES (TAXABLE).

TEN YEN. Give
to Fresh
Air Fund. Determined

as a Surgeon
General Warning:
smoking

like salmon,
he's swum up
the mainstream

to be caught
by camera—a fish
story out

of water, hooked.
Sinker. Loan
shark. Trickle down

etcetera—
his feet
bared & up

with his prices,
propped
on a chair toppled

like big game. The lion's
share. Free trade.
"Hob-nobs

with the hob-nobs"—
blue-chip Basquiat
playing the bull

market, stock-
broken. PESO NETO.
Sell-out

shows.
Whether garage,
rummage, lawn

or fire, such sales
can't last forever—
everything

must go. Black
Monday. Crashing
like a market,

going under—
Basquiat, Ltd
trades drugs

for arms,
swapping junk
bonds, futures.

SIDE A

BECAUSE IT HURTS THE LUNGS

KING ZULU

Louis Armstrong, also known as Satch or Satchmo, for
Satchelmouth, erstwhile Dippermouth, wearing the mask of
the King of the Zulus in the Mardi Gras parade, New Orleans,
1949. Many civil rights spokesmen, for all their professed
pride in their black African heritage, were downright scandal-
ized when the long-since-renowned Armstrong declared that
being chosen for such a role was the fulfillment of a lifelong
dream. But perhaps they confused the ritual role of the Zulu
King of Mardi Gras with that of minstrel entertainer. In any
case they seem to have overlooked the fact (as a home-town
boy would not) that the specific traditional ritual function of
the outrageous costume and conduct of the King of the
Zulus is to ridicule the whole idea of Mardi Gras and the
Lenten Season.

[ALBERT MURRAY]
STOMPING THE BLUES

NATIVE CARRYING SOME GUNS, BIBLES, AMORITES ON SAFARI

He love this world
with its overworked
mercies, its igloos

& the not-so-
insignificant
salaries—POACHERS

PROVISIONS
MISSIONARIES. He done
paid, full,

for the rain-sweated
streets—TUSKS GOD KIN—
these tropics,

his jangled head
of hair. Some bad
vines. I WON'T EVEN

MENTION GOLD.
(ORO). So, tough guy,
lessee what you got:

ten fingers counting
thumbs, a leg
over everyone—ROYAL

SALT INC ©—
& a million
midnights heavy as he

maybe can carry.

TOBACCO VERSUS RED CHIEF

He has remained
on bartime — borrowed — set
just ahead

in order to shut
up early — Sorry
Kemosabe, we're close — last

call, Mohican. Maroon.
Make that
a double — lines

them up & knocks
them down. What's left
to want? We aren't —

he's got it all
figured out — How —
his problems fire-

water to walk —

JIM CROW

He need remedy
—MISSISSIPPI—is on
the edge—cutting—

has got to tame
take it off like a mask
or a prom

dress. Quick. Hopeless.
He's just
cause, a 24-hour pharmacy

he be—what else
to say? Swaying,
no use denying

what his body
craves—the beast
of his back—hunched

begging. WARNING:
Content
Under Pressure—

O the aisles
& aisles of his drugstore
mind—pain

relievers, cheap sun-
glasses, flesh
colored band-aids & Easter

candy overstock
he wants to ingest, fill his form
with—aerosal spray

Do Not Store Near Flame
to keep what's bug-
ging him away—

These milkshaking
counters—Woolworth—he once
could not, down south,

have sat & ordered up
a hot plate
of crow to eat—

LENT

Every day is Lent.
Each day he
giving up

something—meat,
smoke, smack-
crackle-pop—

holding out & forth
for his health.
Every day he gives away

hundreds
to the homeless guy washing
his cabby's window—

Keep the change
to whoever sold
him cigarettes. Each day

is Fat Tuesday, celebrating
something, or the things
that haven't killed us

yet. Each day
is Lent. Each day
giving in

to the skin with its pores
pouring out sweat
lust vomit—every day

he quits. Every day
repents, gives hisself
a second

chance, or given
—like a shotgun bride
wearing white—away.

THE MECHANICS THAT ALWAYS HAVE
A GEAR LEFT OVER

I never understood why when you died, you didn't just vanish, and everything could just keep going the way it was only you just wouldn't be there. I always thought that I'd like my own tombstone to be blank. No epitaph, and no name. Well actually, I'd like it to say "Figment."

[ANDY WARHOL]

NU-NILE {1985}

He's known rivers.

Seen the waves
a fragrant
pomade

laid deep in his hair—
sat down
beneath the barber's chair

& felt the cream
whiten his cheeks,
a straight-edge razor

slapped against leather
cutting his face
like a stash. Gauge.

Roach. SPOONS
SHARPENED TO CUT
FLOUR WITH WHITE

LEAD. He's read
enough to know
the steady undertow

of spleen, drawing
him down—
felt the pain of poison

the flash flood
following heavy veins.
He's no river—

yet rushed
three days to finish
the Palladium's

Mike Todd Room,
a mural wide
as Mississippi

—NOTARY© —
seen the crowns
of the Congo, drums

like tins of hair grease
PETROL OIL
fighting crocodile curls,

a conk's tears.
He's laid down, spent,
beside the Lethe

& seen the sunset
come & sunrise & still
his eyes open, riveted—

thought himself dead
till he heard his own
blood's ebb. His skin sold

—grown thin—downriver.

COLLABORATIONS {1984}

ARM + HAMMER
Warhol sets Basquiat
like a chain
smoke, or gang, to work

painting beside Warhol's brand,
his Arm
& Hammer. B kneeling

in white, abuzz, the two
doing an African master-
piece together. No sickle,

no Mao now —
B draws his seal encircling
another negro, this time

brown.
COMMEMORATIVE
crossed out, a coin

coming up heads.
ONE CENT. The black
bars across the frame

a censor's—
from our hero, the negro
's mouth, a horn

dangles like a pipe.
Let's call
a spade

a spade.
Could be Bird.
Could be

B blowing it
again, to coin
a phrase. Chump

change, two
bits—above the date
1955 in jailblock

letters: LIBERTY.

SOCIALITE
RUBBER RAT.
RUBBER
RAT. The head

of Spiderman
floating
EYE EYE

TEETH—
behind Your Friendly
Neighborhood

the headline
SOCIALITE
FIFTH AV

DEATH LEAP
hand-drawn
by Warhol, slinger

of webs—*Where are you
going to Spiderman
Nobody knows*

who you are—
social butterfly
—LEECHES—scaling high

rises, Empire.

ALBA'S BREAKFAST
ABC's—Andy
Warhol, Basquiat
& Francesco Clemente

surround a table, empty
bowls, day's supply
of vitamin D.

Paint on plates
TOAST EGGS
BACON COFFEE

"   FAST SPECIAL"
"M*GR PLEASE."
B's close-cropped

hair, elegant
in well-starched
shirt, black jacket

like flak. Bullet
proof, bus
boy—Short

Order Cannibal
Wanted.
Draws a head

beside Clemente's
mouth open
his wife ALBA©

ALBA. For his own
face, Warhol places
—"L*T M* GO"—

a machine, washing.

NEGRESS

Black bars
—a supermarket
code across her chest

—R.SGS TMK—
hair flipped
like a 60s girl-group

Felix the Cat
grinning, going
wild—

How-To
for a bow-tie.
Some of my

best blacks
are my friends.
STEEP INCLINE

GIN—B
& W standing
beside the painting

not smiling. ZENITH.
1/2 1/2 1/2 —
good help is hard

to bind — your waiter
for today — silhouette,
servant — *Gin-Soaked*

Critics panning
like fool's gold
— SHOT GLASS — the show.

EVERLAST
Mismatch — FIXED

FIGHT — black
turtlenecked
Warhol in shorts, white

wig. ROBE. GLOVES.
GLASS.
JAW. Bare-chested

Basquiat, fists
cross his chest
as if at a wake,

his own. LADIES
+ GENKS. WHITE
TRUNKS. In this

coroner — the challenger —
his hair
electric, posed

with W's mitt
mashed against his face
facing-off. RABBIT

PUNCH. Combination,
jab, upper
hand—EVERLAST

on both belts, going
toe-to-toe. After
making the rounds—

Shafrazi + Bischofberger
present—promote—
the critics weigh in

B OOOOO
& the show don't sell.
B retreats, splits

—decision—
won't take no seconds
SMARTENING UP A CHUMP

no lip.

HIS GLUE-SNIFFING VALET

Prodigy, prodigal
son—he's sick
of being called

Warhol's protegé,
lap dog. Mascot.
Lawn

jockey. Negro
for Hire—avail.
for promos, parties

public
& private. Inside
like a joke

a job, he tires
of his titles—
bad boy, cash

cow, emblem.
SCALO MERCI
on an elephant's

trunk, tusks
blunted—he just cain't
seem to forget.

Trouble the water.

The Cajun—
visitation, visage—
bares his teeth

from a wheelchair,
his valiant friend
behind him

bellowing for change,
begging. Shoulders
OATS like a wt. *Wade*

in the water, children—

Withdrawal.
B recoils, draws
back, then paints

the pair all night—
*His Glue-Sniffing
Valet.* Lackey.

Understudy.
Bridesmaid. Media
darling—*It's all over*

but the crying.

Takes the *Come*
painting, glue
gooey, that Andy gave him

—a rare bird—
& gave it away
or burnt it

but good. *Bridge
o'er trouble water.*
O to be young

gifted & black
balled! enfant
terrible—smackhead—

an equal opportunist
destroyer. Harmful
if swallowed. Brat,

bat boy, idiot
savant. Read
the fine print—Not

responsible
for loss damage
delay or Acts

of God. *God
don't like ugly*—
And He ain't stuck

on pretty. Boy
Friday. Sunday
painter, Tuesday child,

Yesterday's news.
Rock cried out—
no hiding place.

Johnny come
lately (if
ever). Jack

of all trade.
What's-
his-face.

LIGHT BLUE MOVERS {1987}

This tag not
to be removed.
Fit

to be tied
& gagged—
B rages

tossing
his cookies,
his art out

the window—
THE WHOLE
LIVERY LINE

BOW WITH THIS—
Basquiat case
bouncing off walls

padded with paintings
done in
his 8 hundred dollar

straitjacket
& tie—LUCKY
TO HAVE MY CANVAS SUIT

DRYCLEANED
BEFORE THE RIOTS.
He's ruint

—?;#@*!?!—
another pinstripe Armani
another painting

forsaken—not
for sale—
defenestrated. LIKE THIS

THE BIG MONEY
ALL CRUSHED—
Neighbors drag

some works in out
the rain—washed
up—salvaged

from his hip
wreck. Some show
up, days later,

at his dealer—
ALL CRUSHED
INTO THESE

FEET. Full
of bile, black,
yellow

—ill-humored—
his blood
Type A, boiling

like seas. EDGE
NOT REWORKED—Boy
Friday on Island

Manhattan (sold
for twentysome
clams & a handshake)

made USA. He's gone
from 100 Prince
to Great

Jones (right
above Bond), left
far behind his first dealer

& her basement
where, drugged up,
he worked—one day leaving

her no note, just
unfinished canvases
slashed like tires—steeling

himself—THESE FEET—the hood
ornament on a Cadillac
some swift, unseen

fingers freed.

ANTAR

Mouthful
of stars, cold
sores, tooth

not yet gone—
his gapped grin
like Rousseau's

Sleeping Gypsy—
the rainbow
hair & cloak

at which Lion sniffs
curious
patient. Hungry.

Gravy. Will he
wake? We want
him to & don't

want to know
what might devour
him—King

of Jungle, Lord
Beast.
Signifying

Monkey throwing
down doo
doo. Blue

night. Talking
shit—Hey Lion,
Elephant say he cd kick

your ass like a bad
habit—jive-end-
jive—say you're a chump

or dead. Or both.
All them
lies. Makes you see

stars, wish some cold
could rain & lick
these bones away—

WARHOL ATTENDS ROY COHN'S FINAL BIRTHDAY PARTY
AT THE PALLADIUM, JUNE 1985

Welcome, won't you sit
down sir, the whole
world's here. Who's she

with? What's he think
he's wearing? Warhol dishes
the guest list, giving

friends dirt the next day.
Cohn in the crowd, center,
feeble but no one

asks. From the walls
monitors lower
the boom—Cohn

back in the day, cheeks
full. Bald. Bow-tied.
Dozen-faced. Speaks

about Red Tide, those pinkos
in the Cabinet. Closet
cases. Names his black

list, where we're all
guests. Domino effect—
Warhol thinks back to the Love

Boat where he played
himself—was the nine hundred
ninety-ninth guest—

his snapshot beside Isaac
the black bar-
tender, the mermaids, the party

where they paraded
past guests cursed to appear
in the life preserver

who'd since died—Ethel Merman,
Peter Lawford, Slim Pickens—
then the lucky thousandth

guest announced! Where is
Warhol's name on the roll?
Balloons fall like dirigibles

the cake battleship-big
covered in Old Glory. Singing.
Candles blown out

with some help Cohn rises
to talk, thanks, the years
have been good—

from the rafters God
Bless America & the shredded
plastic flag unfurls—

Cohn soon dead, secreted
like the dark hair, buried
awkward, beneath Warhol's wig.

LAST SUPPER {1987}

It went
well, as expected,
& here you are

Mr Warhol, awake
with your fear
of hospitals, gall

bladder gone—
though Bob Robert (not his real
name) signed in

it was Andy
who went under, out,
Andy whose insides

—gangrenous, snaking—
got opened up
again. Sewn. New

scar to match
his missing
spleen, half

a lung—the shooting
pain, now ancient, still
shown on his skin.

Andy did you
think of death
or did it think

of you? The woman
under long dark
hair, seemed to follow

him across Europe—
She's trying to do
me in! It took time

a lot of talking
to calm
your nerves. Flew

back two days early
for the operation
& here Warhol is, his

extra parts missing
like his clothes—no bladder
or tape recorder,

just the television
overhead
like God. Talking.

The private nurse is nice.
No thanks,
I'll eat later—

Warhol in the place
he dreads,
that h-word

he can't even say
much less
be driven past, avoided

since he was shot.
TRUSS CORSET
TRACTION. He's read

every thing he was
brought
or tried—*Dreamgirl*

& the gossip
columns, *His Way*.
BE A SOMEBODY

WITH A BODY. Eat
something. Shoot
you up to stop

the pain — Warhol
sitting up
on a quiet ward.

The walls sky.
Future open as his side,
healing. Am I

the most famous
person admitted?
Should he

do more *Last
Suppers?* All Italy
seemed to love them—

storming in
when, across the street,
DaVinci's lines

were too long. Thousands
crossed the Corso
Magenta to see

the refectory full
of your latest
silk screens—

bikes revving
behind the Big C
like Hell's

Angels, price
placed over
Christ's head—

6⁹⁹. *Dove*
soap. Bread. Monocled
Mr Peanut,

a lung in a top-hat
tapdancing—
GE—we bring

good things
to life.
Where's that nurse?

It's late. REPENT
AND SIN NO MORE.
Warhol needs

ARE YOU "DIFFERENT"?
something like attention.
HEAVEN

& HELL ARE JUST
ONE BREATH AWAY!
No prayer or Hail

Mary can help—
THE ONLY WAY
OUT IS IN.

The nurse from Avalon
asleep or deep
in her Bible—Paul,

Romans, Revelations—
Warhol alone on
this white wing,

growing stiff as a brand
new bill—fifty,
a hundred, a face

fading green.

GRAVESTONE {1987}

Breaking ground.
Root
work. Dirt

nap. Trip-
tych—three doors
unhinged. Pearly

gates. Our boy's
done lost it—
Warhol's gone.

For good. Staring
walls, skulls—
Basquiat paints

Andy's elegy—
~~PERISHABLE.~~
PERISH-

ABLE. Post-
mortemism.
Factotum

pole. Green
thumb. Grounds
keeper. Boo

hoo doo—
floor crawling
with art, Uncle

Andy's Ant Farm.
DT's. Bottled up
djinnis. Cartoons.

Finger food.
B bawling, crash
& burn. Rose.

Ghost story.
Skeleton
key. Anno

Domini.

Going to funerals is a good way to remember who's dead. I try
to avoid funerals, but if you don't go to them it's easy to forget
who's in heaven—acquaintances die and three months later
I'm back to asking people how they are.

ANDY WARHOL'S PARTY BOOK

MEMORIAL MASS FOR ANDY WARHOL, APRIL FOOL'S DAY, 1987

Some say he's a saint
Others he's not
dead yet

That that robot
from Japan
made a perfect match

Or a facsimile
laid in state
That he's changed

his name
& moved Upstate
Whatever they say

one thing's set—
Andy's out
of it, his phone's cut

he can't be reached
Some say
he's a ghost

That he's only gone
to Bloomie's
shopping

Think what you want

Andy's not
here, didn't get
an invite

& is more
than upset
His former assistant

Gerard Malanga
wears the front-
page of the *Post* —

ANDY WARHOL DEAD
AT 58
silk-screened on a T-shirt

Andy's kaput
& loves
this fuss, the mass

of people, the host
every last
minute

Front row, Basquiat's
sorrow-shot,
all salt

COLLECTION OF DENNIS HOPPER {1987}

HEART AS ARENA—
Hopper in a docu-trauma
discussing Warhol

after his own comeback,
seated before
his giant Basquiat—

PROMETHEUS.
BLACK TEETH.
Andy's already bit

the dust
& Basquiat's just
about to—DEBT (SIC)

PISS PASSPORT
FREE KIT LIGHT RED
PAYING DUES.

Since Hopper's
debut he's lived
hard & died

none—seen
the best stars
of his degeneration

deep in reef-
er madness.
RELIGIOUS

TALK GETS FREE
MEAL. EROICA.
THE OBSERVATORY

FROM THE JAMES
DEAN MOVIE—
behind him

a beaten brown
head blurts out
VICIOUS DOG   EAR WAX

POURING POWDERED ROCK
OR EARTH OF VARIOUS
COLORS AND PAINTING

FOR A SICK CHILD.
Hopper's hairline
has made only a brief

retreat—widow's
peak—much the same
ATOMIZED

SHRINE SKULL
as when Warhol
painted him in a ten-gallon

hat, whisky smile
as in his *Last Movie*
which wasn't. ALCOHOL

IN THIS TOWN
SENATE INVESTIGATION
CHAMPION SHIP BOUT—

wears that same squint
seen in *Giant*
or *Rebel without*

a Cause—
JAWBONE
OF AN ASS

BIRD
OF PARADISE—
Jimmy Dean rolling

out the cliff-bound
car, T-Bird or Mercury,
just before it soars—

SAVOY

To tango
To solo
To jump

Jim Crow
To wallflower
To twist again

like we did
WATERCOOLED
last summer

To dance card
& contest
To shake

it to the east
the west
To split

To ain't got
that swing
To two-

step
To swig
SHINING SHOES

IN ST. LOUIS
SHINING SHOES
IN ST. LOUIS

To can-can
ENGINE, GAS
To last

request
To toot-toot
tootsie

goodbye
To dip
RIBBON RELEASE

To tap
HEY! HEY!
HYENA

BABOON
To Eagle Rock
To turkey

trot
"Snakehips"
To horse

around
ASCENT
To regret

To forage
& forget
COLLECT

ALL 12
To nickel
& dime to death

FLIES FLIES
FLIES FLIES FLIES
FLIES FLEAS

To jive
To jig
To rent

party & flop
wally
To shim-sham

shimmy
To shag
To speakeasy

Get off that dime!
To cut
a rug, slow

drag, Charleston
Lindy Hop
To cakewalk

DECOMPOSITION
OF WATER
"JOHN

THE REVELATOR"

To God
& part
way back

SATCHMO

SIDE A —
the face handled
careful, black

wax grooves
going round
in an endless

endless grin —
King Louie
Armstrong

blowing like no
tomorrow.
Oooh hoo

I wanna be
like you-who —
Pops wipes his brow

with a kerchief
as if cleaning
a needle, a skipping

dusty LP.
An ape like me
would love to be

human too.
SIDE B —
his bull

horn muffled,
sounding fog —
labels spun

202

too fast
to read. Heebie
Jeebies. *Is*

you is or is
you ain't —
Satchelmouth

Old Scratch,
between the devil
& the deep

blue sea — his Hot Fives
scat, out-play
Beezlebub on a good

day — two horns
twisted
up out his hair —

STARDUST

Lady sings
the blues
the reds, whatever

she can find—
short
changed, a chord—

God bless
the child
that's got his own

& won't mind
sharing some—
"BILLIES BOUNCE"

"BILLIES BOUNCE"
Miss Holiday's up
on four counts

of possession, three-
fifths, the law
— locked up—

licked—the salt
the boot—refused
a chance to belt

tunes in the clubs—
ex-con. Man,
she got it

bad—Brother
can you spare
a dime

bag. MEANDERING
WARMING UP
A RIFF—

she's all scat,
waxing—
SIDE A

SIDE B
OOH
SHOO DE

OBEE—
detoxed, thawed
in time

for Thanksgiving—live
as ammo, smoking
—NOV. 26 1945—

Day cold as turkey—

THE MECHANICS THAT ALWAYS HAVE A GEAR LEFT OVER {1988}

Horse-back
in the photograph,
on the wagon

again, wearing
a grin & one
of those fake Foreign

Legion hats,
flaps in the back
against the heat. Have-

locks. Gone
to Hawaii to kick
his habit & not

the bucket—
wasted not
wants not.

Brought
an expedition of free-
loaders, given

away, as Papa
would say, the store.
VENTA

TOTAL—
the sharking
shore—

THE WHITENESS
OF THE WHALE
AFFADAVIT CHART

JONAH HISTORICALLY
CONSIDERED —
The lone negro

on a lifeboat
— moral center — MONKEY
ROPE — go ask Canada

Lee or Jo. Singleton
Copley —
SHARK SHARK

SHARK SHARK.
His crew
has struck gold,

land, lightning.
Jackpot. Wind
fall. WHY

THE THUNDERBOLT KILLS
A DOES NOT
WOUND HIM —

They've held on
for the ride
of Frankenstein.

A made man.
TWIN STAR
RACING STYLE

TWIN SEAT TWIST
OF TOBACCO —
He gives

good bank.
FREE
(FOR A LIMITED

TIME ONLY).
His nature
nurtures—

green leaving
his hands
WHITE GLOVES

NO. 73
faster
than fingernails.

Don't matter—
another day,
another drawing

sold — failed sketches
found crumpled
in his trash— rifled

through, picked,
auctioned off. High
bidder. LABORATORY

TESTED
FOR STRENGTH
MOUTH TESTEDd

FFO R
ESTHETICS.
Sick

of the bloody
city — man
overboard — SHARK

SHARK SHARK.
Only oils draw
him back — stretched

on linen, covering
it all, almost
"ANY BROKEN COIL"

with a blue
so sky
he could stay there —

CHARLIE CHAN ON HORN

For Prestige

Bird records
a few sides
(for contract

reasons) as Mr Charlie
Chan—no matter
the name his blues

sound the same,
same alto blaring
ALCHEMY,

licks exotic
as *Charlie Chan
in Black Magic*—

Chan's dark sidekick
Birmingham Brown
(a.k.a. Man-

tan Moreland)
seeing ghosts,
fleeing. *Feets*

do yo stuff—
THRIVING ON A RIFF,
Bird on a run

(in one place)
eyes bugged out
blowing

like Gabriel.
Solos snorted—
in one nose

& out the other.
Gone. Number one
son—don't they know

Charlie Chan
is a white man?
Fu Manchu too.

(Bless you.)
Parker play
your horn, not

no coon
no coolie in a white
suit. Bird's shot

his way to the top—
made a fist, tied off
& caught

the first vein
out of town.
Laying tracks—

NOWS THE TIME
NOWS THE TIME
BIRD GETS THE WORM—

Now dig
this—Basquiat
lit, lidded, does

a gravestone—
CPRKR
in the Stan-

hope Hotel,
the one Bird bit
the dust in (ON AIR)

high. TEETH.
HALOES
FIFTY NINE CENT.

Who knew how well
Basquiat would follow—
feet (six deep) first.

OUT GETTING RIBS

You can see lots of self-fulfilling prophesies in his work, or in the work of anybody whose work runs deep. I don't think Andy did the *Last Supper* because he planned to die. I don't think Jean did the *Man Dies* painting in his last show because he planned for that to be his last show. He loved to live, as you can tell. But maybe the more you love it and the better you do it the more resistance you encounter. Especially if you work all the way.

Creating his last show was an ordeal for him because he wasn't well and he was in an almost paranoid state about the serious "dis" that he was getting from certain quarters of the art world. Lots of people wanted him to fall. It made me sick. I can only imagine how he felt. But his sick was better than most people's well, and the last time I dreamed about him he said he was felling [sic] much, much better.

[GLENN O'BRIEN]

RIDING WITH DEATH {1988}

The bit
of bones beneath
him, reined—

he mounts
Death
's bleached back—

a brown body out-
lined on linen.
SPINE. TORSO. SIN

HUESO. He's
too through
with this merry-

go-round—the clowns—
the giant stuffed
animals to win

or take your picture
with—the pony rides
& overpriced

food. *There's always
a unicycle.*
His hands turned

forks, tuning,
feeding what hunger
held him together

this long. Trawling
his own stomach.
Tripe. The snipe hunt

he's begun has come
up empty—left holding
the bag—trick,

nickel—this cat's
gotten out, crossed
the path. Curious—

his horse
turned back
from our foxhunt,

this possum run.
Given in—SAMO©
AS AN ESCAPE

CLAUSE—found face
down
like a payment.

And we who for ages
whaled, blubber
& wonder

why he's thrown
ashore, rowed
himself here

hallelujah—answered
out the blue
whale some unseen

call. A siren—
the ambulance
racing a sea

of cars—*emergency*—
family only
beyond this

point—our fists
against his breath-
less chest.

UNDISCOVERED GENIUS OF THE MISSISSIPPI DELTA

From Hazlehurst
       Mississip's
Most Diversified County

From Hazlehurst
       Center of Copiah
Down Hazlehurst way

He split like
       a boll weevil
wanting no part of no

COTTON
       ORIGIN OF
P. 4

picking only
       that guitar of his
cross every jook

in the Delta—
       music his alpha
& omega —his Satan— he slid easy

like the neck of a guitar
       IV: THE DEEP
SOUTH 1912-1936-1951

Only thing easier
       was picking women
NEGROES

NEGROES
       UDDER
NEGROES—

Find you the ugliest
         pug ugliest
woman in town

Love her & she'll
         treat you swell—
Awww wouldn't we

have a time babe—
         He made a killin
each town he played

shacking up
         with a lady
who'd get him

three squares, hot—
         A DIET RICH
IN PORK PRODUCTS—

THE "COW" IS
         A REGISTERED
TRADEMARK—

then ramblin on.
         FIG 23: cigarette low
from his lip—

Married secretly
         & didn't much care
whether a lady

be spoken for—
         Even better
if she was—

no strings.
		He blurred them chords
He wed the underworld

blessed by corn—
		NO MORE
MULES

& crossroads.
		He'd play
till nothing was dry

no throat nor eye—NEITHER
		SWORD NOR SPAR
DISPERSED INTO THE FOUR

CORNERS OF THE EARTH—
		got chased
out of town more times

than he could count—
		A. SICKLES
B. MATTOCKS

C. FORKS
		D. AXES
Hear them dogs closing like a train.

Each lady knew
		he was singing
for her

Every hand knew
		it was his gal who
that Johnson boy was crooning to—

Played his home
          town, flirting
with trouble, wife

of the jook joint's owner—
          · sipped bottles unsealed
thinking them kisses

She winked & he winced
          He took him another
swig, kept on singing—

MISSISSIPPI
          MISSISSIPPI
MISSISSIPPI MISSISSIPPI

SLAVE SHIP—
          the poison's sicksweet clutch.
EL RATON.

Hellhounds—heels—

Soon couldn't stand
          stopped his number
to stumble outside

1. EAST
          2. WEST
3. NORTH

ground spinning
          like a cotton gin.
PER LB. 49¢.

NOSTRILS
          JAW TEETH
LARYNX

SIDE VIEW.
1. Place of Death
Greenwood (Outside)

2. Full Name
Robert L. Johnson
3. Sex   *M*

4. Color or Race
B
5. Single, Married, Widowed,

or Divorced (write
the word)
Single

7. Years
26—
the dirt deep around

Three Forks,
the jook clearing out
Serves him right

Sho you're right
18. Burial,
Cremation, or Removal

19. Undertaker
Family.
His strong

heart held on
four days before
the poison colded him —

in his chest
          a train
derailing—

before the blues caught
          up & hounded him
MARK TWAIN

MARK TWAIN
          MARK TWAIN
TWAIN

out his cotton pickin mind.

NATURE MORTE {1988}

KING PLEASURE—
a crown drawn
over the ING —

be, pie, see, th—
all good ends
deserve begin

nings. His success
is ful—
remorse, mourn,

thank. It's the last
inning, winning
run on third

—so what's
the hitch?
Hooked

on phonics, canvas
orange as caution,
slow—treading light

ly—His days
lettered, spelt
out. Counted

like syll
-ables, -ogisms. Votes.
Vetos. Give us the dirt,

the pudding-proof—
child-, fire-, fool-
—keeping up

with his jonesing.
It's all Greek
to him—alpha

omega—paint
turning to words
& worry.

We want the scoop
the skinny—
this jig on a jag

the nig who would
be king.
Who can B

trust? -ed, mis-,
-worthy—
he's been written out

& off. Pronounce-
d dead. MOST YOUNG
KING GET THEIR

HEAD
CUT OFF. Here
is the low

down deal
the dope—Full
of tions

(*read:* shuns)—
situ-, tempta-
frustra-

—he be all
suffix, all after
& -likes—

life, child, dis, un

SOUL

Given up
a life
of falsetto

fuzzy hats
& funk
soundtracks

to find God—
Rev Green
on the good foot

gone back
to singing the gospel
before soul—

sanctified—baptized
by a pot
of boiling grits

grafted to his skin—
pressed—re-issued
from the original

masters—Aretha
Franklin & blind
black musicians—

both Ray & Wonder.
Praise
the Lord & please

give to the Fraternal Order
of Wheelchair-Bound
Black Singers

—a moment of silence—
Pres. Curtis Mayfield
& Teddy

Pendergrass, Vice-
—gone is the life
of ladies'

panties thrown
like a voice
onstage, going

gold. Pledge now
to the Association
of Shot

Soul Singers
& Last Words
—Sam Cooke, founder—

Bitch, you shot me

slumped in a chair.
What's going on?
What's going on? Co-

founder Marvin Gaye gunned
down by God—
his father

the right reverend—
the son—holy—*O*
Mercy Mercy Me—

poor Donny Hathaway
five stories
up, mistaking plain air for

a walk across water

RIDDLE ME THIS BATMAN

Doesn't everyone die
a dozen
times, ready

or not? ZLONK!
KAPOW! @;#$%*!?!
The cancer

slow, or sudden
as heart's failure—
desire desire—whether

suicide or mass
murder, we all
share final

breath. Rites.
Residuals.
To the Batetcetera

Robin! driving
crazy, the panicked
power pole he wraps

his car around—
is ours,
that last prayer, even

if only a shopping
list, some milky
thing. *Must*—

reach—
utility—
belt—too many

spinoffs in the works
too many arch-
villains going

makes things easy for.
HO HAHAHAAHAHAA
HEE —hear

them now.
Reruns. Side
kicks. So riddle

this, Batman—
with the water
in your tank rising

risen, the sharks
unfed, slandered
& anxious

what tricks lie up
your mask? what
geniusy grab-bag

will you open
after this word
from our sponsor?

LINK PARABOLE

Now back
to our show, to our
question marks & fish

hooks—what
suffering shark
repellent

Batty, what holy
torpedoes
will rescue you

high, dry?

EROICA {1988}

BEAM: TO LOOK
BEAN: - TO SUN
BAT: AN OLD OLD

WOMAN
MAN DIES.
MAN DIES.

AIRCOOLED
CONDENSER
BAGPIPE: 1940S

VACUUM CLEANER
B.O.A.C :   BUREAU
OF DRUG ABUSE

CONTROL
BALE OF STRAW: WHITE
BLOND FEMALE

BALL & CHAIN: WIFE
BALLOON ROOM:
PLACE WHERE

MARIJUANA IS SMOKED
MAN DIES. MAN
DIES. MAN DIES.

BALLS: TESTICLES
BAM: (FROM BAMBITA)
BANANA: ATTRACTIVE

LIGHT SKIN
BLACK FEMALE
BAND: WOMAN

BAND: JAZZ
BANG: INJECTION
OF NARCOTICS

OR SEX.
MAN DIES.
BANJO: INSTR

FRM WEST
AFRKA
BANK: TOILET

TNT
(—6H₂ CH)
MORNING GLORY

SWEET POTATO
MAN DIES.
MAN—

FOR BLUES
FIXIN TO DIE
BLUES

BARK: HUMAN SKIN

MONK

Melodious Thunk

   his wife called him & here
      he is, hammering
the piano keys

   HARDHEAD
      HARDHEAD
HARDHEAD

   like a heart—fingers
a flatted fifth
   slapboxing the baby

grand. See him
   spinning round
like midnight, or

   like his middle
      name, Sphere—
From here

he seems almost typing,
   tapping out
   "Evidence" on the ivories

like a recorder
   for the court. Hear
ye, hear ye—

Monk holed up, holy, in Minton's
   smoky basement.
   Nine-month engagement.

Underground, bunkered
down, his unsteady pace
    around the place makes its way

into our heads—he debunks—
    can't stop
    the sounds from seeping out

    his skull cap.
NERVOUS SYSTEM.
    "THEIR HEADS WRAPPED."

O, bring it back—

    that "Ugly Beauty,"
"Epistrophy," that four-cornered
    hat—

    GOING TO HEAVEN.
MY APOLOGIES.
    Piano lid

lifted like a coffin's,
    Monk swaying
    again at the piano

    as if on the moaner's bench
in church. His foot
    sweeps the floor

    DRIED FLOWERS
DRIED FLOWERS
    DRIED FLOWERS

DRIED FLOWERS
DRIED FLOWERS
     SINGING FEET

searching for the invisible
    brake, or
        the car

accelerator, urging us on.

SKIN HEAD WIG {1982–83}

So we are walking
And the dead
  And the dead

down Haight
Street, looking
  And the dead

for the day
for nothing particular—
Beneath concrete

the beach!
someone's written
under our feet—

the dunes long gone
from mixed
marriages to shops

selling the Summer
of Love, vintage duds
  And the dead

On the corner
some sidewalk
sale, junk—

a victrola
WORKS
the owner doesn't really

want to part with
PURE
ALL BEEF

piles of old
Playboys, dogged,
Miss April missing

And the dead—
COMIC CODE
AUTHORITY

NO. 33—
Among Men
at Work & The Police

we find The Offs
album, cover
chalk on black

board—THE FINAL
BATATTLE
SMOKE

BOMB—recognize
your hand Basquiat
your halo

IBID.
IBID.
your white triangles—

No one believes
it's you
    And the dead

No one buys
you're here
on some punk's

sidewalk—
MOST PEOPLE TRY
TO GROW

HAIR THIS IS JUST
THE OPPISIT—
We pay

the skinhead
two bones
for the record—

MADE OF FLESH
TONED LATEX
WILL FIT—

Old Glory
tattooed to his arm,
boots laced

like stitches
to his knee,
an oxblood amputee

FOR THE EXECUTIVE
WHAT WOULD LIKE
TO CHANE

HIS APPEARANCE—
Turning the album
over we see

a man with a gun-
tattoo aimed
at his head

past
your name
  And the dead

And the dead—

PENTIMENTO

Old paint on canvas, as it ages, sometimes becomes transparent. When that happens it is possible, in some pictures, to see the original lines: a tree will show through a woman's dress, a child makes way for a dog, a large boat is no longer on an open sea. That is called pentimento because the painter "repented," changed his mind. Perhaps it would be as well to say that the old conception, replaced by a later choice, is a way of seeing and then seeing again.

[LILLIAN HELLMAN]
Pentimento

DOS CABEZAS 2

We are the walking
wounded in war
movies who insist

Go head
without us—
so on

youse went—

Now we forget
what the fight
was for first

place—ANTONIUS SEPTIMUS
FIRE OF CARNIUS
ASCETICISM—Last leg

of the relay
race & medals weight
down our chests

without a limb
to pin them with.
HOMER

ILIAD TROY
ACHILLES—
You are a ghost

itch, the knee we
no longer have
& have

learned to live
without. What we bare-
ly miss. Being

behind is sometime
worse, the survivor
's curse

& cure: remember . . .

MAN STRUCK LIGHTNING—2 WITNESSES

Hell is no help.
Here, unharrowed,
hurried, you are before

your time, some
sacrifice up in flame—
lamb, lion, monkey

up a tree.
You're early. We
still run on

CPT—taking
sweet our time
—form a single line—

getting around
to you—
Your mama.

Thou art
in the ante-
chamber of after

—the Big Below—
downtown in this
City of Dis

where your ears
from our words
must burn—

ANYBODY SPEAKING WORDS

Nothing can breathe
you back. Not
the long work

of drink, cocktails
at six, beer,
whatever, whisky,

Old Granddad, Crazy-
horse. SPORTS. The dull
sweet white wine taste

of morning. Nor
the eastward walk
past St Mark's

& Auden's marked
house, past
the park, skip

rope of streets no longer
numbers, into the Nix
the Nada — to cop

the coin-sized, -colored
bags. Squats. The poor tarred
streets, corners piled

with boys & beggars.
Smoke smoke. OPERA.
Your faraway father

in his suit
coat of silence. Your mouth
mock-moving on

its own. NOTHING
TO GAIN HERE. Gone,
nothing can stir—

ERNOK

AWOL, SNAFU, VIP
You done
been abbrev'd—

sent into the DMZ
history—
RIP, VFW

BFD—bearing
left, nitro-
glycerine

in yr trunk
TNT, FDA
you pkged yourself

special 4th
class rate
snuck past the drug

sniffing dogs
at Bureau Tobacco
& Firearms

under siege
the influence.
Stamped rec'd.

COD. JFK. MLK. BOOSH-
WAH-ZEE OR CIA?
You come to us piece

meal—LSD, AC
DC, BCBG, OD,
DOA—under cover

the mask the gun
to produce—
BSQT 83, JMB

on the hook
the take. NFS. HNIC.
MOMA, CBGB'S—

it's anyone's guess
what all
you stand for. PS—

remittance req'd
w/in 30 days
RSVP ASAP

"REPLICAS"

And after all this
time, guess who
decides to show

up—through—
your paint
thinning as you

once feared
—as your hair never did—
the head behind

CHKN appearing,
the face beneath
the halo—pentimento—

going the way
of nothing else on earth:
returns. CAST IRON

AUTOMOBILE REPLICAS.
You are ex-
cavated, communicated—

the faces pressing
from beneath the painting
—X-RAY GLASSES—

giving a glance
of what's past.
DRY GOODS

ACTUAL SIZE
NEGRO SPIRITUALS—
What the ghost wants

is not always
obvious—knocks
as if it knows

who's hidden
or why—please, one
momento mori—

*AY ALLAH ENLA*G* Y*U
M*Y ZEUS E*LARGE YO*
    BUDDAH EN*A*GE *OU—

Better this life—grief—
beyond death
than the death-in-life—

GRI GRI

You are what
's missing—
the spook we have

not seen—haint
haunting
—what's that—

STERILE DESTROY
AFTER SINGLE
USE. No matter

what vévé
we make, what
tobey we take

as totem, the b-b-
bogeyman gonna
get us—some spirits,

like likker, never rest.
If only
the left side

of the equation weren't
true: what does not
make you stronger

will kill you. Go ask
the vermin behind
the fridge—nuclear

survivors, roach
motel fine diners—
this house falling

around you—the mice—
no piper to pay or play—
poltergeists rattling

their chains like dice—

PEGASUS

I met Jean-Michel Basquiat a few days before he died. Before or after, it doesn't really matter.

[DANY LAFERRIÈRE]

THE DINGOES THAT PARK THEIR BRAINS WITH THEIR GUM

Once he died they went in
& took out everything—
paintings,

of course, some unfinished—
others the wavy wary
walk of the end—more

Basquiat saved & liked
(not in that order)
like *Jack Johnson*

that sang to him. Those got kept.

They say they took his
entire record collection,
platter after platter

he'd spent years
& dollars collecting
while the rest of us

went crazy for mirrored
one-sided discs
that, lighter, cost more

& sounded almost
worse—LPs & 78s
& 45s bought like scag

from a regular source
on the street—dark
discs he once held like a note

& loved—

& just left
them on the curb,
roadkill for anyone to pick.

Folks did. Eroded.
Within days
nothing was left—

EXPENSIBLE.
GOING TO HEAVEN.
MY APOLOGIES.

Like to think not all
sit silent in a landfill
the way we one day will.

Like to think some
weren't sold, piece
by bit, or bulk

for 50¢—that some
some soul saved
& at night slips

out their bent
sleeves like a magician's—
the needle

placed against the dark
that like a planet spins—
BILLIES BOUNCE

BILLIES BOUNCE—
till sound spills out
& for a side

at least—unless the arm
resets, repeats—
we taps

our tired feet.

EPITAPH

You done blown
this taco stand
sky high, AMF

under earth,
an oath. Caught
the first thing

smoking. PARA
MORIR. Gone
with summer-

time
& the living
is easy. High

cotton.
You weevil
why'd you

weave us?
Stitch yourself
back like a spider

or under-
taker—
give up the car

service that waits
& waits while you
paint—it's too

much—will drive
you to your grave.
DEC 1960

AUG 1988 —
your date
kept, no chance

to grow fat
& useless — no
names please —

GREENWOOD.
You stay
thin & dead, a language —

maggot:
n. 2. *an extravagant*
notion, whim — ants

for angels, eyes —

SHRINE OUTSIDE BASQUIAT'S STUDIO, SEPTEMBER 1988

Back on Great
Jones
his face

against the façade
fronting the carriage
house rented

from Warhol—
inside, his suits
stiffen from starch,

spilt paint.
He's bought
the farm whole,

enchilada
& all—August
& the heat

covering everything,
needle-sharp,
asleep. No more

feeding
his habit art—
he's gone

& done it
this time, taken
his last dive.

Exit, stage right.
A broken
record—his black

skin thick,
needled
into song—

a swan's. Upon
graffitied brick—
INSIDIOUS MENACE

LANDLORD
TENANT—
folks pile

candles flowers
photos notes
to God & lace—

anything TO REPEL
GHOSTS, keep
his going at bay

before memory comes
early, snarling
& sweeps him

into the mouth
of euphemism—
sanitation worker, waste

management engineer,
garbage man, dumpster
diver, trash

heap, heaven.

HEAVEN {1985}

Can we get
a Witness
Protection Pro-

gram like you
did? Sent
into hiding, secret

identity, altered
ego as if Clark
Kent. Don

some glasses & that
is that. AUTO-
PORTRAIT.

DEAD BIRD©.
Awww
next time Boss

you *play Superman*—

convince everyone
it's him committing
the crime, not you

on a diamond spree
trafficking—
him who's taken

wing—ASCENT
FLESH
SPIRIT

*Geez Boss
it was only
a fin*

(police whistle)

—Next time it'll be
a Mickey Fin.
You slipped

*U*ERMA*
duped & downed
like a drink.

Who'da thunk
you'd end up
amnesiac, new

name & no way
home? Under
our yellow sun

—class A star—
your powers
failed—up

up away—
too much krypt-
onite kept

in a lead box

even your x-
ray specs could not
penetrate

or name. CYCLOPS.
MOTIONLESS
AIR—MIRROR MASTER

ANOTHER
SATISFIED COMB
USER. Your cape

a shroud
a shrug—RIBBED
WING PARTLY

COVERED IN SILK—
in sky
bird plane

faster loco-
motive smoke.
A*ION COMIC*—

You're up
—& out—there
somewhere, making

it safe for all.
(NEGRO
SPANIARD). CRANK

like a call—
Can we
get a wit-

ness? VICE;
a President, something
votive to see

& save us, say,
spin the earth
alternate universe

Mr Mxyzptlk.
This piece of blue
kryptonite—or red—

has a diff. effect
each time. Bizarro—
SOJUZ PLODO

sometime you grow
six limbs—count—
others it strikes

you down, slow
—no Lois, no Jimmy
Olsen to pick

the lock & set
you free—Super-
dog, Supermonkey

Supercat & -horse

who live on the moon.
HEAVEN©.
Can we get some

witness? Come on
into the shun sine
Superboy—

say something.
Anything. Spare
us this silence

—fortress solitude—
this invincible
bulletproof blue—

TWO PHOTOGRAPHS OF JEAN-MICHEL BASQUIAT, PARIS

1988
Face all
tore up
from the smack

he's stark
staring
clutching Kerouac

to his chest—
The Subterraneans
edition as beat

up as he looks. His last

show & promo—
around his neck
the bolero—

its boxer getting
licked, strung
out, face giving way

DESPUES DE UN PUÑO

or his own fist
raised
in defense

defiant—laced
tight. Arm up
like a slot

machine's—BAR
BAR BELL—he's hit
jackpot, his eyes

have it—looking
something
like starlight

(far-off, half-
dead already)
hand covering one eye.

1986
Bare
chested, the noose
like a Texas string-tie

casual, loose—
black
tie affair. Lasso

lariat, he's at
the end
of his yoke—

pulling the horse
before being carted
off. Monkeying

around. He's both
the tree—banyan
or baobab—

& the hanging
man. Gallows
humor. Tongue-

tied. One day his luck
will run out
like his friends—

let's hope long after the dope does—

close call, cropped
hair—suppose he dries up,
then out, gets

clean & finds God—

Let us help
him sip *café
au lait*, laughing

beside the still waters.

THE NINTH CIRCLE

In a back booth
Mingus, Chas. is upset
    that Lenny Bruce

keeps using the word *cunt*
    in this his last act, uncut—
Mingus sitting up front

    with the critics, the shrinks
who each set and session
    hand him drugs—he's checked

hisself into Bellevue,
    a ward without
no way out. *All the Things You*

Could Be by Now
    If Sigmund Freud's
Wife Was Your

Mother. The thick haze
    of Camels and buddha—
The Black Saint & the Sinner Lady—

    in this halfway house
to heaven. *Oh Lord Don't Let*
    Them Drop that Atom

Bomb on Me. He's the life
    of the after party, setting
like a jet, slapping that upright

    till he bleeds—onstage, caps
on other player's bits—
    You got no tone—scats

and bangs the piano with his fist.
        They didn't teach us to talk,
says Mingus. He's not pissed, just

        paces, speaking a blues streak.
Puffs a pipe, intellectual-
        like, blowing smoke

shooting off his rifle
        —the kind that killed
Kennedy —like a mouth. *This mule*

        could be called
stubborn & lazy
        But in a clever sort

of way, this mule could be
        waitin & learnin & plannin
for a sacred kind of day —

        SEMI CIRCLE OF DAMNATION.
DIGESTIVE TRACT.
        CIRCULATORY SYSTEM. PAN-

LUNARISM. Evicted
        from the Great Jones school
he built and planned—

        his cool
has gone—cries
        as his bookcases and dreams pile

along the curb. *My country*
        Tis of Thee, Sweet
Land of Slavery —

Mingus thanks the cops,
says he thinks
        they're trying to help

as they put him in the cruiser, booked
        for unknown pills, blues,
an empty syringe. No dope. Onlook

        as the city reposesses
the beds and books,
        even his bass

        put under lock—
Mingus cracking up, in pieces
        like chess. Rooked.

Onstage wearing his African "dress"
        Mingus wields
the neck of his bass

        like a bottle—
a fifth
        of gin—or a battle

axe. *The Shoes*
        Of the Fisher-
Man's Wife Are Some Jive Ass

Slippers. Before
        Lou Gehrig's disease
grounds him, Mingus's fingers blister

        Better Git It in Your Soul and *Please*
Come Back from the Moon—
        finding that note, exact, his upright's

full bodied, unbowed, half-human moan.

VANITAS

The best *vanitas* paintings contradict themselves. They purport to teach us the emptiness and impermanence of worldly objects while infusing them with transcendent significance and giving them relative permanence.

The modern implication of conceit now associated with the word *vanity* is not present in the use of *vanitas,* the Latin word for "emptiness."

[SALLY FISHER]
The Square Halo

Without you we are
    only words
we manage

to get wrong—
    your name
a death

sentence mis-
    pronounced, u-
nanimous—

Since your lethal
    injection
we have you all

backwards,
    ward back
your zombie, trans

-posed, -lated—
    Even your tag
anagrams to SOMA

—South
    of Market—
the body—DRINK

OF THE GODS.
    Death
has found you

Cuban, victim
    of acronyms—
AIDS, FBI, CIA

OR BOOSH-WAH-ZEE?
    Syllabic
symbolic, psuedonymous—

your name sticks
    with us like Malcolm
Ten, or freeze tag

—you're it—
    kicking cans
playing graveyard. In this grey

game of telephone
    you are on
the fritz—the lam

—911—dis
    -connected,
-missed.

Asleep
    you count
black sheep

bah, bas-
    relief—
receding with each

touch. Our
    sweat spoils
your face. You are what

we say of saints,
    assumed—
Your name, mis

-placed, -took
    echoes
about the room.

RELICS

He had to live up to being a young prodigy, which is a kind of false sainthood.

[KEITH HARING]

THRONE
See his chair
everywhere —
first against

the wall or
beneath René
Ricard's portrait —

THE GREAT UNWASHED
GOTHIC PAINTING
BLEACHED ASSASSIN CURATES

MILAGE OVER A DISTANCE —

B money
squatting, in color
— UNBREAKABLE —

it's there
in the corner, the throne
not yet torn

SLAPPING SENSE
IN TERMS OF TICKING
SUITCASES

DENIES EVER SEEING —

crouched yellow
& black beneath
canvases waiting

to be covered.
KING PLEASURE
leans the wall

besides @#$%&*!!
an axe.
In Basquiat's

hands a cigarette
lit, a cup—
paint—

raised to drink,
bless. Toast.
ZZZZZZZ ZZ Z—

Hard to believe
this is where
he once thought & drew—

BRONZE THIS HIGH
BRICK INLAY
EYES IN ANGRY

TO BE ANSWERED—

breath, but here it is
—a fact—& when
no one looks

we sit ourselves & wait

CRAVAT

"Looks like something
you'd clean
your shoes with"

says Our Lady
of Belfast, of Constant
Shyness & she's

right — the tie
that never bound
his neck, bought only

to trade with the assistant
behind Mary
Boone's desk,

is ugly as sin.
Mud-brown, grey,
with red veins

strip-mined down —
it's neither thin
nor wide, time-

less, dated.
MISSONI
UOMO

MADE
WOOL —
price tag still

on, expensive
even now, this tie
points downtown

MANO
MANO
SOHO—

could we still
return this thing
if we want?

MOHAIR
IN SPAIN—
Worn

only once
by the assistant
when he swapped

his tie with Ste
Jean-Michel
of the Perpetual

Deal, Patron
of Paint
& Derelicts,

who in turn took
—looped—the assistant's
bright silk

for a belt—

LOVE
Pink ladies—
a half-gallon
of blues—

large horse-pills
some say add
up to love—

hard to swallow
buy—most just grow
sleepy. A year's supply—

he owns in a jar more
than the city had
before the drought began—

Now love
is a canal, a con-
taminated place—

a word found
on a fridge he painted
when younger

& a smart
someone saved it, took
the door off

to sell—now none will
climb inside
what's left behind

& have it close like
a kiss
or a coffin

BRAIN©
Upstairs,
   Superfly loops on,
      watching the room—

nobody home. *I'm your mama*
I'm your daddy—
Basquiat's 57 Jones

Street pad stands empty
like a tomb
pirated. *Tell ole*

Pharoah, let my people go.

Laboratory
lobotomy—
he's cooking

with grease, his
brain pickled
as if a mummy's

(pulled out slowly, bit
by bit, with a hook
then stored

honeyed, in small jars).
Shine
sir? on his knees

yassah yassah
painting—
HEAD

OF A FRYER
SARCOPUGUS
OF A PHYSICIAN.

The boot
black stand
piled high upon

the grey
    matter of boxes,
        color xeroxes—

The sign
    for salt
        —a tesseract—

drawn on a soap
    box. PODIUM. SUB
        COMMUNICATOR—

Upstairs, Priest wants
    out of the Life
        giving up

white women & fur
    for piece
        of quiet. ONE WOMAN'S

MAN. A YOUTH
    WITH "CROW" SYNDROME:
        (AN ATTRACTION

TO SHINY OBJECTS),
    little plastic men
        with parachutes, LPs

line the room—
    HUMAN ANATOMY.
    WORLD HISTORY.

PARADE/RIOT.
    HUMAN HEART
        HUMAN HEART™

Packrat, pickup
   artist—
      he's saved everything

cept hisself.
   NEW CONFESSIN' THE BLUES
   DEPRESSED PALSY TV—

By the time
   we find it, enter
      unknocked

like the PO-LEEECE
   —freeze—
      the place

has changed like a mind—
   someone tipped him
      off & our boy's split—

his magpie
   nest turned
      to cold storage

for vegetables—
   radishes & cabbage & Chinese
      noodles, dirt-brown potatoes

with one hundred eyes, winking.

ONE MAN SHOW

Apples, orangutans—
on Lafayette, below Shinbone
Alley, Basquiat is high

up, muraled, sprayed against
the scapula-shaped bldg
in his (now) famous

VanDerZee pose. *(Trans:*
"By the Sea.") Today the city
is someone familiar

round every corner.
Spartacus 1960. Upper
View. Brains

& radiant
babies in the No
Man's Land north

of Haring's Pop
Shop. *Never Eat*
Pork: Their Golden Rule.

This mural's garish
colors do not suit
but stay—least

longer than you
managed to. Apology
apostrophe—

you sit bored, called
for jury duty,
condemned—tenement

testament man.

CANONIZATION
You died days
before St John
the Baptist (his

beheading)
on a day of sun
sans music—a

capella—
you have joined
them, the patrons of ores

& Bohemia—
the ones with altars
& metals

& occassions.
St Martin
de Porres (interracial

justice & hair-
dressers)
who sold hisself again

& again to gain
money for the church—
able to appear

& disappear, power
of aerilization
(hence patron

saint of television)
would have been proud.
You are our St Ides

of March, that talk
behind
your back—

Et tu, Judas?

to which we
bow, reply, like Moses
the Black

of Abyssinia, dead
your same day
(Byzantine calendar)

born a slave, committed
the most heinous
crimes & then converted

(means not known).
Met by marauders
& martyred

when he would not save
himself by force—
"The Ethiopian Hermit"

known in his life
for his extreme
mortifications. DANGEROUS

NEIGHBORHOOD.
In what state
did you lay? How

long? DOUBTFUL
DOUBTFUL — Come
let us pray.

Let us kneel to Benedict
the Moor, to all
the Black

Madonnas, let us kiss
the cross
of Crispus Attucks' arms—

LANGSTON HUGHES

LANGSTON HUGHES
LANGSTON HUGHES
  O come now
   & sang
them weary blues—

Been tired here
feelin low down
  Real
  tired here
since you quit town

Our ears no longer trumpets
Our mouths no more bells
  FAMOUS POET©—
  Busboy—Do tell
us of hell—

Mr Shakespeare in Harlem
Mr Theme for English B
  Preach on
  kind sir
of death, if it please—

We got no more promise
We only got ain't
  Let us in
  on how
you 'came a saint

LANGSTON
LANGSTON
  LANGSTON HUGHES
  Won't you send
all heaven's news

HENRY GEDZAHLER: *You got rid of your telephone a while ago. Was that satisfying?*

J-M BASQUIAT: Pretty much. Now I get all these telegrams. It's fun. You never know what it could be. "You're drafted," "I have $2,000 for you." It could be anything. And because people are spending more money with telegrams they get right to the point. But now my bell rings at all hours of the night. I pretend I'm not home . . .

MAKING IT NEW

URGENT TELEGRAM TO JEAN-MICHEL BASQUIAT

HAVENT HEARD FROM YOU IN AGES STOP LOVE YOUR
LATEST SHOW STOP THIS NO PHONE STUFF IS FOR BIRDS
LIKE YOU STOP ONCE SHOUTED UP FROM STREET ONLY

RAIN AND YOUR ASSISTANT ANSWERED STOP DO YOU
STILL SLEEP LATE STOP DOES YOUR PAINT STILL COVER
DOORS STOP FOUND A SAMO TAG COPYRIGHT HIGH

ABOVE A STAIR STOP NOT SURE HOW YOU REACHED STOP
YOU ALWAYS WERE A CLIMBER STOP COME DOWN SOME
DAY AND SEE US AGAIN END

RETROSPECTIVE

In the dark, the nasty
night, mother of million
nights, you return

looking, not for fame
but ducats, not begging
but collecting

on what was
owed you, getting back
what you sharked.

Lien.
Let us guess
JMB—you can see

everything clear
as your complexion,
as composed. COWARDS

WILL GIVE
TO GET RID
OF YOU. Even when

your skin gave in
to the heroin, you still
looked young & beautiful—

yet you confess
you feel much
better now, got

a handle on things,
the drugs fled on
out, left cold

turkey. THE SKY
IS THE LIMIT©.
Wings

& white meat.
Spleen still
missing, but not

quite missed.
If only
you'd said so

long like a television
station, signed off
the air—Star

Spangled Banner
blowing before bars—
red, yellow,

more—color—
before brief
black—the static—

LINER NOTES

In treating Jean-Michel Basquiat's work and life—a distinction his so-called critics have often blurred—we have consulted many sources. A complete bibliography would be far too long & missing the point, especially for an artist who appropriated & copyrighted as many images & sayings as he created. Moreover, this is not a biography, but an extended riff—Basquiat and his work serves as a bass line, a rhythm section, a melody from which the poems improvise. I did not know Basquiat; I do now, through his work. Most important to a full grasp of his life is to see his paintings live.

Some helpful references: The Whitney's *Basquiat*, edited by Richard Marshall; Henry Gedzahler's 1983 interview with the artist, found in *Making It New*; Vrej Barhoomian's black market *Basquiat*; Phoebe Hoban's "SAMO© . . . Is Dead: The Fall of Jean-Michel Basquiat"; and *Basquiat Drawings & Notebooks*, roughly in that order. Greg Tate's "Flyboy in the Buttermilk" is one of the earliest and still one of the best writings on Basquiat; of the growing number of articles on the artist since then, one from the British *Guardian* stands out as a rare, balanced and accurate piece of journalism.

To give a visual idea of Basquiat's hand, SMALL CAPITALS generally indicate painted/drawn text found in his work. Titles often correspond to paintings; the dates following titles apply to the work and are included to indicate a sense of the history of the art & artist. (Dates are *not* the dates of my composition). Basquiat, in the context of the seeming casualness of his canvases, put it best: "Everything is well stretched even though it looks like it might not be."

As might be expected, a show about Basquiat includes "found" text & imagery. The following list includes those things not common knowledge or property:

7 Campbell's Black Bean Soup: *for Ellen Gallagher*. The quote a *nigger's loft* taken from *The Andy Warhol Diaries*, ed. Pat Hackett.

8 Poison Oasis: To be read *al dente*, slowly.

10 Bros. Sausage: During one of his many attempts to run away from home, Basquiat went to a state park. He soon returned.

29 Defacement: Michael Stewart, graffiti artist, was killed by New York's finest for spray-painting in the subway.

36 VNDRZ: James VanDerZee, photographer, documented famous and local Harlem figures from the 1920s until his death in 1982,

a year after he photographed Basquiat. His name means "by the sea."

41 Jack Johnson: In the voice of the first black heavyweight champion of the world, tried for "white slavery" under the Mann Act. For further reference, we suggest *Bad Nigger!*, his autobiography *Jack Johnson Is a Dandy, Jack Johnson & His Times*, and Arthur Ashe's *Hard Road to Glory*. Also "The Black Hamlet" from *Sports Illustrated*, 1959. Miles Davis recorded the score (& wrote liner notes) to the eponymous 1969 documentary, narrated by Brock Peters.

77 Amateur Bout: "Limited to 1000 shrinkwrap copies. Editorial & design supervision by Gerard Malanga."

87 Saint Joe Louis: Gentleman Joe pictured in the corner of a room, slight slouch, by photographer Irving Penn would seem to be one inspiration for this painting. The snakes in BSQT's title refer to the Brown Bombers managers and others—for Louis, tho he made millions, in the end welcomed folks to Vegas from a wheelchair & died impoverished.

109 Peruvian Maid: *for Danny Rimer.*

117 Quality Meats for the Public: *griots,* the philosopher-poet-historians of West African groups, were revered yet not buried with the rest of the tribe—instead they were left in trees for the buzzards.

122 Self-Portrait as a Heel, Part Two: Los Angeles was also the scene of comedian/shaman Richard Pryor's accident in which he suffered third-degree burns and almost died after freebasing. Pryor, currently suffering from MS, now says it was self-immolation.

124 Coke®: *white girl* is street slang for cocaine.

133 Vocabulario: By all reports, Basquiat spoke impeccable Spanish, having lived in Puerto Rico when younger.

135 Onion Gum: To be read up tempo, *al forte.*

141 Oleo: Bert Williams ("Uncle Eggs"), famous light-skinded comedian who performed in blackface, the first black person in the Ziegfield Follies. "Wait till Martin comes," meaning Go Down, Death, quoted in *Harlem Renaissance.*

145 Revised Undiscovered Genius: Bill Traylor, former slave, was a self-taught artist who began painting in his old age in Mobile, Alabama.

183 Antar: Rousseau refers not to the philosopher, but rather the self-taught artist, Le Douanier, called so by his artist friends (Picasso among them), because he worked at a post office.

185 Warhol Attends Cohn's Final Birthday Party: Roy Cohn served under McCarthy & was a rabid anti-communist, helping send the Rosenbergs to the electric chair & blacklisting/destroying many a career.

Though gay himself, he often persecuted others for their sexuality. He was also the lawyer for the owners of Studio 54—who later went on to open the Palladium— while they were under investigation for, and ultimately convicted of, tax evasion. Cohn died of AIDS in 1986.

187 Last Supper: Warhol died from complications after routine gall bladder surgery. In the previous year he had shown a series of Last Supper paintings, silkscreened from a cheap copy of DaVinci's painting. He also executed a number of Last Suppers painted by hand, something Warhol had not done in two decades, but had taken up again in his collaborations with BSQT. These last paintings often include apocalyptic phrases from religious or psuedo-scientific flyers handed out on the street.

206 The Mechanics: Go see Alfred Hitchcock's *Lifeboat,* and John Singleton Copley's painting *Watson and the Shark.*

210 Charlie Chan on Horn: *for John Yau.* Since recording this single, we have learnt that CHAN appears in many a painting; Chan was also the name of Charlie Parker's wife.

224 Nature Morte: Found in a painting, KING PLEASURE is a jazz vocalist known for rendering scat & vocal "translations" of jazz tunes.

227 Soul: *for Eisa Davis.*

231 Riddle Me This Batman: *for the late Jerry Badanes,* joke teller and inspiration, who passed away suddenly during the composition of this canto. The Bat represents both a sign of life and of death: Batman always in peril, about to die cliffhanger style; yet always saved, vampiric, nocturnal, death-defying.

232 Eroica: Latin for "heroic," "Eroica" also is the name of Beethoven's 3d Symphony, originally for Napoleon Bonaparte, later for "the memory of a great man." In his research, Kevin Young realized that the definitions listed in the painting most likely came from Clarence Major's groundbreaking *Dictionary of Afro-American Slang,* from 1969.

252 Gri Gri: The title refers not just to a painting but to a protective charm in certain hoodoo cultures.

255 Pegasus: Besides the winged horse from Greek mythology, and a bonus track I never could finish, *Pegasus* is also the title of a large late painting, done in *chiaroscuro,* with what appear to be hundreds of small symbols in black on a white ground. Standing before it, one marvels at the time, effort, and concentration, the sheer horse-power involved. At the top of the painting, large black swaths of paint have begun to descend like night, or a mood, threatening to cover the entire canvas. How many of Basquiat's canvases have

another *Pegasus,* or its multitude of symbols, buried beneath layers of paint? Whither destruction and creation? Who knows what has already been lost?

260 Epitaph: AMF is slang for "adios, motherfucker," taken from a painting. In this same early *Untitled* (1981) work, found in the Rubell collection, GREENWOOD & PARA MORIR appears in an uncannily prophetic vision of B's death & burial in Greenwood cemetery seven years later.

262 Shrine Outside Basquiat's Studio: If you look closely, you can still see the graffito *Je t'aime Jean-Michel* written on his Great Jones Street doorbell.

272 The Ninth Circle: the name of a Village bar bassist-composer Charles Mingus frequented. See the double memoir *Mingus Mingus.*

278 Relics: THRONE: Refers to a chair that Basquiat once owned now in the hands of a collector; indeed, it can be seen in the background of a late 1980s photo of the artist. CRAVAT: *for Stephen Frailey,* who sent me the necktie in question. BRAIN©: *CURTIS/LIVE!* at The Bitter End, NYC: Mighty Mighty (Spade and Whitey), I Plan to stay a Believer, We've Only Just Begun, People Get Ready, Stare and Stare, Check out Your Mind, Gypsy Woman, The Makings of You, We the People who are Darker than Blue, (Don't Worry) If There's a Hell Below We're all Going to Go, Stone Junkie. ONE MAN SHOW: The mural of Basquiat, located on Lafayette around the corner from the artist's Great Jones loft, was painted over a few years ago.

292 Retrospective: To be read *misterioso.*

AMF

A NOTE ABOUT THE AUTHOR

Kevin Young is the author of six collections of poetry and the editor of Library of America's *John Berryman: Selected Poems*, the Everyman's Library Pocket Poets anthologies *Blues Poems*, and *Jazz Poems*, and *Giant Steps: The New Generation of African American Writers*. His book *Jelly Roll* was a finalist for the National Book Award and the Los Angeles Times Book Prize, and won the Paterson Poetry Prize. His collection *For the Confederate Dead* won the 2007 Quill Award for poetry and the Paterson Award for Sustained Literary Achievement. *Dear Darkness* won the Southern Independent Booksellers Award and the Julia Ward Howe Prize. The recipient of a Guggenheim fellowship, Young is currently the Atticus Haygood Professor of English and Creative Writing and curator of Literary Collections and the Raymond Danowski Poetry Library at Emory University in Atlanta.

www.kevinyoungpoetry.com

A NOTE ON THE TYPE

The Hoefler Text and Hoefler Titling families of typefaces, designed by Jonathan Hoefler, were designed to celebrate some favorite aspects of two beloved Old Style typefaces: Janson Text 55 and Garamond No. 3. Unwittingly, the names "Janson" and "Garamond" both honor men unconnected with these designs: Janson is named for Dutch printer Anton Janson but is based on types cut by Hungarian punchcutter Nicholas Kis; Garamond is a revival of types thought to have originated with Claude Garamond in the sixteenth century but were in fact made a century later by Swiss typefounder Jean Jannon. Hoefler Text and Hoefler Titling are published by Hoefler & Frere-Jones at www.typography.com.

COMPOSED BY
Creative Graphics, Allentown, Pennsylvania

PRINTED & BOUND BY
Offset Paperback Manufacturers, Dallas, Pennsylvania

DESIGNED BY
Gabriele Wilson